"As an evangelical Baptist who share ⟨...⟩ salvation, I naturally welcomed this su⟨...⟩ ⟨...⟩ ⟨...⟩ celebrated preacher's theology and how it applies to the Christian life. But I also resonate with Michael Reeves's deep concern that Spurgeon be read by a much wider audience than his coreligionists. Responsible for a veritable torrent of words, most of which remain in print a dozen decades after his death, he is one of the great Christian authors of the nineteenth century. And it is only right, therefore, that he be known and read by that wide audience of evangelicals who love his Savior. This book is a tremendous place to start: a draft of refreshment from deep Spurgeonic wells—just what is needed in our day."

Michael A. G. Haykin, Professor of Church History and Biblical Spirituality, The Southern Baptist Theological Seminary

"Ask people what first comes to mind when they hear the name Charles Spurgeon, and they will invariably answer with something about preaching. Indeed, Spurgeon is widely considered 'The Prince of Preachers,' and deservedly so. But he is so closely identified with powerful preaching that many fail to realize what an eminently godly man he was. Yes, Spurgeon pastored the largest evangelical church in the nineteenth-century world. Yes, his collected sermons extend to more than sixty-three thick volumes, sermons which continue to sell well today. Yes, his fame as a preacher made Spurgeon the most famous name in Christendom during his lifetime. But he should be equally known as a man of deep piety and a vibrant Christian life. Thankfully, Michael Reeves helps rectify Spurgeon's reputational imbalance with his book *Spurgeon on the Christian Life.* Superbly researched and winsomely written, it demonstrates how Spurgeon—in sickness and in health, in success and in tragedy, in the public eye and in the home— sought to live a Christ-centered life according to the Bible. Whether this is your introduction to Spurgeon or he has been a hero of yours for decades, you will be encouraged by this book."

Donald S. Whitney, Associate Dean and Professor of Biblical Spirituality, School of Theology, The Southern Baptist Theological Seminary; author, *Spiritual Disciplines for the Christian Life* and *Praying the Bible*

"With accurate and careful brushstrokes, Michael Reeves paints for us a three-dimensional portrait of the preacher and leaves us chanting with Helmut Thielicke, 'Sell all that you have and buy Spurgeon.'"

Christian T. George, Curator, The Spurgeon Library; Assistant Professor of Historical Theology, Midwestern Baptist Theological Seminary; editor, *The Lost Sermons of C. H. Spurgeon*

SPURGEON

on the Christian Life

THEOLOGIANS ON THE CHRISTIAN LIFE

EDITED BY STEPHEN J. NICHOLS AND JUSTIN TAYLOR

Augustine on the Christian Life:
Transformed by the Power of God,
Gerald Bray

Bavinck on the Christian Life:
Following Jesus in Faithful Service,
John Bolt

Bonhoeffer on the Christian Life:
From the Cross, for the World,
Stephen J. Nichols

Calvin on the Christian Life:
Glorifying and Enjoying God Forever,
Michael Horton

Edwards on the Christian Life:
Alive to the Beauty of God,
Dane C. Ortlund

Luther on the Christian Life:
Cross and Freedom,
Carl R. Trueman

Newton on the Christian Life:
To Live Is Christ,
Tony Reinke

Owen on the Christian Life:
Living for the Glory of God in Christ,
Matthew Barrett and
Michael A. G. Haykin

Packer on the Christian Life:
Knowing God in Christ,
Walking by the Spirit,
Sam Storms

Schaeffer on the Christian Life:
Countercultural Spirituality,
William Edgar

Spurgeon on the Christian Life:
Alive in Christ,
Michael Reeves

Warfield on the Christian Life:
Living in Light of the Gospel,
Fred G. Zaspel

Wesley on the Christian Life:
The Heart Renewed in Love,
Fred Sanders

SPURGEON

on the Christian Life

ALIVE IN CHRIST

MICHAEL REEVES

WHEATON, ILLINOIS

Spurgeon on the Christian Life: Alive in Christ

Copyright © 2018 by Michael Reeves

Published by Crossway
        1300 Crescent Street
        Wheaton, Illinois 60187

Cover design: Josh Dennis

Cover image: Richard Solomon Artists, Mark Summers

First printing 2018

Printed in the United States of America

Unless otherwise indicated, the author's Scripture quotations are from the ESV® Bible (The Holy Bible, English Standard Version®), copyright © 2001 by Crossway, a publishing ministry of Good News Publishers. Used by permission. All rights reserved.

Scripture quotations marked KJV are from the King James Version of the Bible.

Emphases in Scripture quotations have been added by the author.

Trade paperback ISBN: 978-1-4335-4387-6
ePub ISBN: 978-1-4335-4390-6
PDF ISBN: 978-1-4335-4388-3
Mobipocket ISBN: 978-1-4335-4389-0

Library of Congress Cataloging-in-Publication Data

Names: Reeves, Michael (Michael Richard Ewert), author.
Title: Spurgeon on the Christian life: alive in Christ / Michael Reeves.
Description: Wheaton: Crossway, 2018. | Series: Theologians on the Christian life | Includes
   bibliographical references and index.
Identifiers: LCCN 2017026030 (print) | LCCN 2017032366 (ebook) | ISBN 9781433543883 (pdf) |
   ISBN 9781433543890 (mobi) | ISBN 9781433543906 (epub) | ISBN 9781433543876 (tp)
Subjects: LCSH: Spurgeon, C. H. (Charles Haddon), 1834–1892.
Classification: LCC BX6495.S7 (ebook) | LCC BX6495.S7 R44 2017 (print) | DDC 286/.1092 [B]
   —dc23
LC record available at https://lccn.loc.gov/2017026030

Crossway is a publishing ministry of Good News Publishers.

VP   28   27   26   25   24   23   22   21   20   19   18
15   14   13   12   11   10   9   8   7   6   5   4   3   2   1

For John and Joan,
with deepest love and gratitude
for the best gift I have on earth

CONTENTS

SERIES PREFACE

Some might call us spoiled. We live in an era of significant and substantial resources for Christians on living the Christian life. We have ready access to books, DVD series, online material, seminars—all in the interest of encouraging us in our daily walk with Christ. The laity, the people in the pew, have access to more information than scholars dreamed of having in previous centuries.

Yet, for all our abundance of resources, we also lack something. We tend to lack the perspectives from the past, perspectives from a different time and place than our own. To put the matter differently, we have so many riches in our current horizon that we tend not to look to the horizons of the past.

That is unfortunate, especially when it comes to learning about and practicing discipleship. It's like owning a mansion and choosing to live in only one room. This series invites you to explore the other rooms.

As we go exploring, we will visit places and times different from our own. We will see different models, approaches, and emphases. This series does not intend for these models to be copied uncritically, and it certainly does not intend to put these figures from the past high upon a pedestal like some race of super-Christians. This series intends, however, to help us in the present listen to the past. We believe there is wisdom in the past twenty centuries of the church, wisdom for living the Christian life.

Stephen J. Nichols and Justin Taylor

ABBREVIATIONS

ARM C. H. Spurgeon, *An All-Round Ministry: Addresses to Ministers and Students* (London: Passmore & Alabaster, 1900)

Autobiog., 1 C. H. Spurgeon's *Autobiography, Compiled from His Diary, Letters, and Records, by His Wife and His Private Secretary, 1834–1854,* vol. 1 (Chicago: Curts & Jennings, 1898)

Autobiog., 2 C. H. Spurgeon's *Autobiography, Compiled from His Diary, Letters, and Records, by His Wife and His Private Secretary, 1854–1860,* vol. 2 (New York: Fleming H. Revell, 1899)

Autobiog., 3 C. H. Spurgeon's *Autobiography, Compiled from His Diary, Letters, and Records, by His Wife and His Private Secretary, 1856–1878,* vol. 3 (Chicago: Curts & Jennings, 1899)

Autobiog., 4 C. H. Spurgeon's *Autobiography, Compiled from His Diary, Letters, and Records, by His Wife and His Private Secretary, 1878–1892,* vol. 4 (New York: Fleming H. Revell, 1900)

Lectures, 1 C. H. Spurgeon, *Lectures to My Students,* vol. 1, *A Selection from Addresses Delivered to the Students of the Pastors' College, Metropolitan Tabernacle* (London: Passmore & Alabaster, 1875)

Lectures, 2 C. H. Spurgeon, *Lectures to My Students,* vol. 2, *Addresses Delivered to the Students of the Pastors' College, Metropolitan Tabernacle* (New York: Robert Carter and Brothers, 1889)

Lectures, 3 C. H. Spurgeon, *Lectures to My Students,* vol. 3, *The Art of Illustration; Addresses Delivered to the Students of the Pastors' College, Metropolitan Tabernacle* (London: Passmore & Alabaster, 1905)

Lectures, 4 C. H. Spurgeon, *Lectures to My Students,* vol. 4, *Commenting and Commentaries; Lectures Addressed to the Students of the Pastors' College, Metropolitan Tabernacle* (New York: Sheldon & Co., 1876)

MTP C. H. Spurgeon, *The Metropolitan Tabernacle Pulpit Sermons*, 63 vols. (London: Passmore & Alabaster, 1855–1917)

NPSP C. H. Spurgeon, *The New Park Street Pulpit Sermons*, 6 vols. (London: Passmore & Alabaster, 1855–1860)

S&T [year] C. H. Spurgeon, *The Sword and Trowel* (London: Passmore & Alabaster, 1865–1891)

INTRODUCTION

Crowds lined the streets, hoping to catch a glimpse of the olivewood casket as it made its way through the streets of south London. On top was a large pulpit Bible opened at Isaiah 45:22: "Look unto Me, and be ye saved, all the ends of the earth." It was Thursday, February 11, 1892, and the body of Charles Haddon Spurgeon was being taken for burial. Eighteen years before, Spurgeon had imagined the scene from his pulpit:

> In a little while, there will be a concourse of persons in the streets. Methinks I hear someone enquiring, "What are all these people waiting for?" "Do you not know? He is to be buried to-day." "And who is that?" "It is Spurgeon." "What! the man that preached at the Tabernacle?" "Yes; he is to be buried to-day." That will happen very soon; and when you see my coffin carried to the silent grave, I should like every one of you, whether converted or not, to be constrained to say, "He did earnestly urge us, in plain and simple language, not to put off the consideration of eternal things. He did entreat us to look to Christ."[1]

"Look unto Me, and be ye saved, all the ends of the earth": back in January 1850, those had been the words that had first shown Spurgeon the way of salvation.

> I had been waiting to do fifty things, but when I heard that word, "Look!" what a charming word it seemed to me! Oh! I looked until I could almost have looked my eyes away. There and then the cloud was gone, the darkness had rolled away, and that moment I saw the sun; and I could have risen that instant, and sung with the most enthusiastic

---

[1] *Autobiog.*, 4:375.

of them, of the precious blood of Christ, and the simple faith which
looks alone to Him. [2]

For forty-two years, then, from his conversion to his death, looking to
Christ crucified for life remained the touchstone of Spurgeon's own life
and ministry. Having found new life in Christ himself, he dedicated his
days to entreating all others: "look to Christ."

A Christ-Centered Theology

This is a book about Spurgeon's theology of the Christian life, and those
were the concerns that lay at the heart of it. Spurgeon was unreservedly
Christ-centered and Christ-shaped in his theology; and he was equally insistent on the vital necessity of the new birth. The Christian life is *a new life
in Christ*, given by the Spirit and won by the blood of Jesus shed on the cross.
Spurgeon's was, therefore, a cross-centered and cross-shaped theology, for
the cross was "the hour" of Christ's glorification (John 12:23–24), the place
where Christ was and is exalted, the only message able to overturn the
hearts of men and women otherwise enslaved to sin. Along with Isaiah
45:22, one of Spurgeon's favorite Bible verses was John 12:32: "And I, when
I am lifted up from the earth, will draw all people to myself."

Sometimes Spurgeon spoke of the glory of God as his "chief" or "great"
aim, but that did not in any way temper his Christ-focus or his insistence
on the importance of the new birth. "The glory of God being our chief object
we aim at it by seeking the edification of saints and the salvation of sinners," he explained. [3] "Our great object of glorifying God is . . . to be mainly
achieved by the winning of souls." [4] In other words, as he saw it, the glory of
God is displayed and seen most clearly in God's self-giving through Christ.
God glorifies himself in graciously giving sinners his own abundant life in
Christ through the Spirit.

What I have attempted here is to let Spurgeon's theology of the Christian life shape the very structure—as well as the content—of this book.
This is not a comprehensive analysis of Spurgeon's overall theology, nor is
it a biography, though it should help readers get to know both the man and
the broad brushstrokes of his theology. We will start with a look at the man

---

[2] *Autobiog.*, 1:106.
[3] *Lectures*, 2:264.
[4] *Lectures*, 2:265.

himself, to see how he lived out and embodied his own theology. Nothing so grand as an attempt at a mini-biography—this is more a personal introduction. For in the man himself, so fizzing with life, we see not just a unique personality but an example and personification of the life to be found and enjoyed in Christ. Spurgeon concretely lived out his belief that the Christian life is not a dull, ethereal existence on some higher, invisible plane. It is being more *full*, more *human*—brighter, more involved and more lively. So he would encourage his students:

> Labour to be *alive in all your duties*. . . . Brethren, we must have *life more abundantly*, each one of us, and it must flow out into all the duties of our office: warm spiritual life must be manifest in the prayer, in the singing, in the preaching, and even in the shake of the hand and the good word after service. . . .
>
> Be full of life at all times, and *let that life be seen in your ordinary conversation.*[5]

Then, after a look at the man himself, we will consider the relentless Christ-centeredness of his theology and preaching. After that, we will move to his emphasis upon (and understanding of) the new birth before at last turning to how he saw the Christian life. And at the very center of it all will be a chapter dedicated to his theology of the cross, that blood-soaked throne of Christ and the means of giving us life.

There is something else I have wanted this book to do: to let Spurgeon speak and minister to readers directly. In my own experience, I generally find reading Spurgeon himself like breathing in great lungfuls of mountain air: he is bracing, refreshing, and rousing. I want, therefore, to try to make myself scarce and let Spurgeon leap at readers himself.

And I have a hope for this book: that through it Spurgeon's sermons and writings might be more widely read. Spurgeon is, understandably and quite rightly, a Baptist hero. Yet, a hundred and twenty-five years after his death, his real influence still remains largely confined to Baptist circles. Elsewhere he tends to be treated as little more than a fund of delicious but disconnected proverbs. This, it seems to me, should not be. While I share most of Spurgeon's theology and many of his interests, and was raised just a short walk from Spurgeon's childhood home, I am an Anglican. Spurgeon said of men like me, "I cannot tell . . . how it is these Church of England

---

[5] *ARM*, 188–91. Hereafter, all emphasis in quotations is original unless otherwise indicated.

men are so attached to me. I have said some very severe things about their Church, and yet I have many devoted friends among them."[6] Yes, many of us non-Baptists are his friends. But not many enough. And just as Luther should not be cooped up only among Lutherans, nor Owen among Congregationalists, so Spurgeon should be enjoyed by all. He offers a robustly biblical and thoroughly rounded theology of the Christian life that deserves to be read by all—and all the more for the sheer zing with which he says it.

Spurgeon the Theologian?

And yet, was Spurgeon really a *theologian?* No doubt at all he was a great and influential preacher. In person he preached up to thirteen times per week, gathered the largest church of his day, and could make himself heard in a crowd of twenty-three thousand people (without amplification). In print he published some eighteen million words, selling over fifty-six million copies of his sermons in nearly forty languages in his own lifetime. But none of that is quite the same as to say that he was a theologian. Indeed, some antagonists insisted quite categorically that he was not. According to the Dean of Ripon, who crossed swords with Spurgeon over the question of baptism, Spurgeon "is to be pitied, because his entire want of acquaintance with theological literature leaves him utterly unfit for the determination of such a question, which is a question, not of mere doctrine, but of what may be called historical theology."[7]

With such things having been said about Spurgeon, many were quietly surprised in 1964 when the eminent Lutheran theologian Helmut Thielicke wrote his *Encounter with Spurgeon*, a work in which he commended Spurgeon in the very warmest terms. Really, they wondered, was a self-educated Victorian preacher worthy of the attention of the rector of Hamburg University? It was the beginning of a change that Spurgeon seems to have foreseen: "For my part," he had written, "I am quite willing to be eaten of dogs for the next fifty years; but the more distant future shall vindicate me."[8]

As much as anything, what has thrown people here is the sheer lucidity of his style. He wrote and spoke with such limpid prose, it could all too easily be mistaken for shallow simplicity. But, Spurgeon knew, to think

---

[6] William Williams, *Personal Reminiscences of Charles Haddon Spurgeon* (London: Passmore & Alabaster, 1895), 70–71.
[7] H. L. Wayland, *Charles H. Spurgeon: His Faith and Works* (Philadelphia: American Baptist Publication Society, 1982), 212.
[8] *ARM*, 360.

that difficulty of style is a true indicator of depth of substance is only the mistake of the intellectually proud.

> Brethren, *we should cultivate a clear style*. When a man does not make me understand what he means, it is because he does not himself know what he means. . . . If you look down into a well, if it be empty, it will appear to be very deep; but if there be water in it, you will see its brightness. I believe that many "deep" preachers are simply so because they are like dry wells with nothing whatever in them, except decaying leaves, a few stones, and perhaps a dead cat or two. If there be living water in your preaching, it may be very deep, but the light of the truth will give clearness to it.[9]

Indeed, he believed, such clarity of expression is part of the Christlike humility to which all theologians and ministers of the Word are called.

> Some would impress us by their depth of thought, when it is merely a love of big words. To hide plain things in dark sentences, is sport rather than service for God. If you love men better, you will love phrases less. How used your mother to talk to you when you were a child? There! do not tell me. Don't print it. It would never do for the public ear. The things that she used to say to you were childish, and earlier still, babyish. Why did she thus speak, for she was a very sensible woman? Because she loved you. There is a sort of *tutoyage*, as the French call it, in which love delights.[10]

Almost as damning for his reputation as a theologian was his refusal to dabble in speculation or spend time on peripheral matters. "Speculation," he declared, "is an index of the spiritual poverty of the man who surrenders himself to it."[11] Now certainly he was a man of broad interests, but he lived with such a sense of urgency and such a conviction of the sufficiency of Christ that the need to preach Christ crucified tended to trump worrying over obscure Scriptures or off-center doctrines.

> There is, certainly, enough in the gospel for any one man, enough to fill any one life, to absorb all our thought, emotion, desire, and energy, yea, infinitely more than the most experienced Christian and the most

---

9 *ARM*, 42.
10 *ARM*, 353.
11 *ARM*, 140.

intelligent teacher will ever be able to bring forth. If our Master kept to his one topic, we may wisely do the same, and if any say that we are narrow, let us delight in that blessed narrowness which brings men into the narrow way. If any denounce us as cramped in our ideas, and shut up to one set of truths, let us rejoice to be shut up with Christ, and count it the truest enlargement of our minds.[12]

He is so glorious, that only the infinite God has full knowledge of Him, therefore there will be no limit to our study, or narrowness in our line of thought, if we make our Lord the great object of all our thoughts and researches.[13]

Yet, for all that, Spurgeon was, quite self-consciously, a theologian. Avid in his biblical, theological, and linguistic study, he believed that every preacher *should* be a theologian, because it is only robust and meaty theology that has the nutritional value to feed and grow robust Christians and robust churches.[14]

Some preachers seem to be afraid lest their sermons should be too rich in doctrine, and so injure the spiritual digestions of their hearers. The fear is superfluous. . . . This is not a theological age, and therefore it rails at sound doctrinal teaching, on the principle that ignorance despises wisdom. The glorious giants of the Puritan age fed on something better than the whipped creams and pastries which are now so much in vogue.[15]

Thus, while he was no theological innovator, he sought to avoid superficiality in theology with just the same enthusiasm as he avoided obscurity in communication.

---

[12] *S&T: 1877*, 177.

[13] *ARM*, 53.

[14] *ARM*, 35. Spurgeon's study of the Greek and Hebrew Scriptures is apparent throughout his sermons (for Greek, see *NPSP*, 3:257, 454; 5:287; *MTP*, 8:399; 11:184; 20:209, 237, 441, 500; 24:219; 25:115, 309, 350; 30:58, 514; 32:1, 145–75; 33:184; 36:95, 206, 407; 41:182; 53:324; 56:11, 405; 58:26; for Hebrew, see *NPSP*, 1:224; 2:93; *MTP*, 20:199, 260–61; 21:709; 23:31, 74, 266, 303, 511, 689; 28:400; 32:160, 350, 705; 34:10, 78, 107, 234; 38:407, 470; 56:366). He also referred to a number of Latin works in his sermons, lectures, and commentaries, making it clear, for instance, that he liked to read Augustine in Latin (*MTP*, 25:134; 28:415; 35:190; 37:87). "*The acquisition of another language* affords a fine drilling for the practice of extempore speech," he wrote.

> Brought into connection with the roots of words, and the rules of speech, and being compelled to note the differentia of the two languages, a man grows by degrees to be much at home with parts of speech, moods, tenses, and inflections; like a workman he becomes familiar with his tools, and handles them as every day companions. I know of no better exercise than to translate with as much rapidity as possible a portion of Virgil or Tacitus, and then with deliberation to amend one's mistakes. (*Lectures*, 1:160)

[15] *S&T: 1883*, 125–26.

The notion that we have only to cry, "Believe in the Lord Jesus Christ, and thou shalt be saved," and repeat for ever the same simplicities, will be fatal to a continuous ministry over one people if we attempt to carry it out. The evangelical party in the Church of England was once supreme; but it lost very much power through the weakness of its thought, and its evident belief that pious platitudes could hold the ear of England.[16]

That combination of concerns, for theological depth with plainness of speech, made Spurgeon a preeminent *pastorally minded* theologian. He wanted to be both faithful to God and understood by people. That, surely, is a healthy and Christlike perspective for any theologian. And that is why he is such a rewarding and refreshing thinker.

---

[16] *S&T: 1881*, 39.

PART I

CHARLES SPURGEON

CHAPTER 1

A MAN FULL OF LIFE

In person Mr. Spurgeon was of medium height and stout build. He had a massive head and large features of the heavy English type. In repose his face, while strong, might have been called phlegmatic if not dull in expression. But when he spoke it glowed with animation of thought, quick flashes of humour, benignity, and earnestness and every phase of the emotion that stirred within him. He had many elements of power as a preacher. His voice was of marvellous sonority and sweetness. His language with all its simplicity, was marked by faultless correctness and inexhaustible wealth of diction. He was as far as possible from being a rough or course speaker although he had at ready command a vast vocabulary of homely Saxon words. No one from merely reading his sermons, can form any idea of their effect when delivered. . . . In listening to Mr Spurgeon, one recognised that the chief element of his commanding force in the pulpit was his profound and burning conviction. The message he gave had for him supreme importance. All his soul went with its utterance. The fire of his zeal was consuming, intense, resistless.[1]

Before we wade into Spurgeon's theology of the Christian life, we must get to know the man himself a little. To do that, I want to get behind the public figure to see something of the man's own personality and character. For there is a unanimous and oft-repeated theme found in the witness of those who had personal dealings with him: Spurgeon was a man who went at all of life full-on. He was not simply a large presence in the pulpit. In life,

---

[1] *The Examiner* (New York) (February 4, 1892), 5.

he laughed and cried much; he read avidly and felt deeply; he was a zeal-ously industrious worker and a sociable lover of play and beauty. He was, in other words, a man who embodied the truth that to be in Christ means to be made ever more roundly human, more fully *alive*. In fact, we need to be clear that his liveliness of character, while expressed in ways particular to him, was not a mere matter of unique or inherited personality: it was a natural *but wholly self-conscious* expression of his theology. As he put it,

> We ought each one to be like that reformer who is described as "*Vividus vultus, vividi occuli, vividæ manus, denique omnia vivida*," which I would rather freely render—"a countenance beaming with life, eyes and hands full of life, in fine, a vivid preacher, altogether alive."[2]

> We ought to be all alive, and always alive. A pillar of light and fire should be the preacher's fit emblem.[3]

Mr. Great-Heart

It takes no great insight to see that Spurgeon was a big-hearted man of deep affections. His printed sermons and lectures still throb with passion. At times the emotional freight of his sermon would even overcome him, especially when it was about the crucifixion of Christ. Once, when trying to recount how Christ was then "bruised, trodden, crushed, destroyed . . . sor-rowful, even unto death" he had to break off, saying, "I must pause, I cannot describe it. I can weep over it, and you can too."[4] It was no mere pulpiteer's tactic, though: his private and personal letters to family and friends reveal exactly the same intensity of emotion, and about just the same sorts of is-sues he would address in public.

Perhaps the best insight into Spurgeon's character comes through the introduction he once gave to his equally large-framed friend, John Bost. Calling Bost "a man after our own heart," he gave what amounts to a re-markably revealing *self*-description:

> John Bost is great as well as large. . . . Here is a man after our own heart, with a lot of human nature in him, a large-hearted, tempest-tossed mortal, who has done business on the great waters, and would long ago have been

---

[2] *Lectures*, 2:218.
[3] *Lectures*, 2:221.
[4] *NPSP*, 5:95.

wrecked had it not been for his simple reliance upon God. His is a soul like
that of Martin Luther, full of emotion and of mental changes; borne aloft to
heaven at one time and anon sinking in the deeps. Worn down with labour,
he needs rest, but will not take it, perhaps cannot. . . . [I have] found him full
of zeal and devotion, and brimming over with godly experience, and at the
same time abounding in mirth, racy remark, and mother wit.[5]

This description is revealing in its honest acknowledgment of Bost's (and
his own) depression and struggle. For him, to be "large-hearted," with "a lot
of human nature" in this fallen world does not mean being a triumphalist,
cheerily blustering past all difficulty. Spurgeon could never have done that,
as we shall see in chapter 11. Experiencing life in Christ, the Man of Sorrows, must entail suffering. Yet life in Christ must also involve real cheer,
"abounding in mirth, racy remark, and mother wit."

There were dangers for one so tenderhearted. Spurgeon publicly admitted
that his temperamental sensitivity inclined him to be fearful.[6] Combine this
with his marked generosity in dealing with people, and he could—and did—
sometimes fail in his discernment of character, becoming victim to those who
would abuse his financial openhandedness. Yet tenderheartedness should
not be confused with weakness: along with expressing his love for Christ and
people, Spurgeon could demonstrate a real hatred for wickedness and injustice. Again and again, he spoke of how he would boil with anger at pastoral
abuse, church politicking, and false teaching (especially any form of Roman
Catholicism). And while he surely struggled, it would be wildly misguided
to think of Spurgeon as a fragile pushover. It would be far better to say that
tenderness saved him: it kept his robustness of character from steamrolling
those weaker than himself, and channeled it for their benefit. His blend of
vigor and tenderness made him fascinatingly feisty in showing compassion,
as witnessed by this humor-filled letter of complaint to his publisher:

Dear Mr. Passmore,

When that good little lad came here on Monday with the sermon, late at
night, it was needful. But please blow somebody up for sending the poor
little creature here, late to-night, in all this snow, with a parcel much
heavier than he ought to carry. He could not get home till eleven, I fear;

---

[5] *S&T: 1879*, 68. "Racy" here means "lively."
[6] *MTP*, 36:604.

and I feel like a cruel brute in being the innocent cause of having a poor lad out at such an hour on such a night. There was no need at all for it. Do kick somebody for me, so that it may not happen again.

Yours ever heartily,
    C. H. Spurgeon.[7]

There, both in his care for a socially insignificant minor and in the playfulness of his rebuke, is revealed the man's genial and benevolent large-heartedness. It was an aspect of Christlikeness he wanted to see in all believers, and one he believed essential for pastors: "Great hearts are the main qualifications for great preachers."[8] It was something he would speak about at length with his students, and it is worth hearing him at some length (for both his substance and his style!):

> It is not every preacher we would care to talk with; but there are some whom one would give a fortune to converse with for an hour. I love a minister whose face invites me to make him my friend—a man upon whose doorstep you read, "Salve," "*Welcome*;" and feel that there is no need of that Pompeian warning, "Cave Canem," "*Beware of the dog*." Give me the man around whom the children come, like flies around a honey-pot: they are first-class judges of a good man. . . . A man who is to do much with men must love them, and feel at home with them. An individual who has no geniality about him had better be an undertaker, and bury the dead, for he will never succeed in influencing the living. I have met somewhere with the observation that to be a popular preacher one must have bowels.[9] I fear that the observation was meant as a mild criticism upon the bulk to which certain brethren have attained: but there is truth in it. A man must have a great heart if he would have a great congregation. His heart should be as capacious as those noble harbors along our coast, which contain sea-room for a fleet. When a man has a large, loving heart, men go to him as ships to a haven, and feel at peace when they have anchored under the lee of his friendship. Such a man is hearty in private as well as in public; his blood is not cold and fishy, but he is warm as your own fireside. No pride and selfishness chill you when you approach him; he has his doors all open to receive you, and you are at home with him at once. Such men I would persuade you to be, every one of you.[10]

---

[7] *Autobiog.*, 2:172–73.
[8] *Lectures*, 2:277.
[9] The reference to "bowels" here stems from the biblical notion of the bowels as a center of human affections, especially the feeling of compassion (cf. Col. 3:12 KJV).
[10] *Lectures*, 1:183–84.

A Life of Joy

Spurgeon was an unmistakably and deliberately earnest man. With a deep concern for the glory of Christ and the fate of the lost, he believed that Christians should be able to say with our master, "Zeal for your house will consume me" (John 2:17; cf. Ps. 69:9). Yet earnestness and zeal, for Spurgeon, were *never* to be confused with gloominess and melancholy. It is telling and entirely appropriate that a whole chapter of his "autobiography" (really a biography compiled from his diary, letters, and records) is titled "Pure Fun." For, we are told, "it was felt that the record of his happy life would not be complete unless at least one chapter was filled with specimens of that pure fun which was as characteristic of him as was his 'precious faith.'"[11] It is another reason why he was and has remained so magnetic: Charles Spurgeon was fun.

Entirely upsetting the stereotype that the Victorian era was a long, charmless span of dusty prissiness, Spurgeon's writings ripple with mirth. And evidently even they do not do justice to what he was like in person.[12] The editor of his *Lectures to My Students* would thus be driven to insert attempts at explaining his various impressions and "voices," as he impersonated pompous theologians and fools.[13] Usually, though, one can still sense the humor that cannot quite be caught on a page:

> I would say with regard to your throats—*take care of them*. Take care always to clear them well when you are about to speak, but do not be constantly clearing them while you are preaching. A very esteemed brother of my acquaintance always talks in this way—"My dear friends—hem—hem—this is a most—hem—important subject which I have now—hem—hem—to bring before you, and—hem—hem—I have to call upon you to give me—hem—hem—your most serious—hem—attention."[14]

"What a bubbling fountain of humour Mr. Spurgeon had!" wrote his friend William Williams. "I have laughed more, I verily believe, when in his company than during all the rest of my life besides."[15] Few, it seems, expected to laugh so much in the presence of the zealous pastor; but Spurgeon knew this and seemed to take an impish delight in springing comedy on those around him. Grandiosity, religiosity, and humbug could all expect to be pricked on his

---

[11] *Autobiog.*, 3:339.
[12] William Williams, *Personal Reminiscences of Charles Haddon Spurgeon* (London: Passmore & Alabaster, 1895), 62.
[13] *Lectures*, 1:119.
[14] *Lectures*, 1:133.
[15] Williams, *Personal Reminiscences of Charles Haddon Spurgeon*, 17–18.

wit. Sometimes rather more was broken. Spurgeon enjoyed telling the story of how, as a young pastor in Park Street, he had complained to his deacons about how stuffy and stifling it could get in the building, suggesting that they remove the upper panes of glass from some of the windows to let in more air. Nothing was done about it; but then one day it was found that someone had smashed those window panes out. Spurgeon offered a reward of five pounds for the discovery of the offender, who would then be given the money in thanks. This money the pastor then pocketed, being himself the culprit.[16]

But perhaps it is Spurgeon's cigar smoking that best reveals his sunny playfulness as well as his vivacious willingness to enjoy created things. Personally, Spurgeon found great pleasure in cigars; he argued that the Bible gave him liberty to smoke them, and he believed they helped his throat as a preacher. He was sensitively aware, however, that many Christians felt otherwise, and he was keen not to offend or let them stumble over the issue. When his statement that he smoked "to the glory of God" was printed in the newspapers as if it had been a flippant crack, he was sorry that prominence had been given to what seemed to him a small matter, and quickly wrote to explain:

> The expression "smoking to the glory of God" standing alone has an ill sound, and I do not justify it; but in the sense in which I employed it I still stand to it. No Christian should do anything in which he cannot glorify God; and this may be done, according to Scripture, in eating and drinking and the common actions of life. When I have found intense pain relieved, a weary brain soothed, and calm, refreshing sleep obtained by a cigar, I have felt grateful to God, and have blessed His name; this is what I meant, and by no means did I use sacred words triflingly.[17]

That said, in the right context he would happily use his cigar to replace religiosity with cheerful enjoyment of Christian liberty. William Williams records a day out he took with his students:

> It was a beautiful early morning, and on arriving all were in high spirits—pipes and cigars alight, and looking forward to a day of unrestrained enjoyment. He was ready waiting at the gate, jumped up to the box-seat reserved for him, and, looking round with astonishment, exclaimed:

---

16 *Lectures*, 1:139.
17 Letter to the *Daily Telegraph* (September 23, 1874), cited in Lewis A. Drummond, *Spurgeon: Prince of Preachers* (Grand Rapids: Kregel, 1992), 506.

"What, gentlemen! are you not ashamed to be smoking so early?" Here was a damper! Dismay was on every face. Pipes and cigars one by one failed and dropped out of sight. When all had disappeared, out came his cigar-case; he lit up and smoked away serenely. Astonishment was now on every face. One of the party nearest to him said, "I thought you said you objected to smoking, Mr. Spurgeon?" "Oh no," he replied; "I did not say I objected. I asked if they were not ashamed, and it appears they were, for they have put them all out." And he puffed away quite serenely.[18]

Humor flowed from Spurgeon naturally and freely, but he was acutely conscious of both the power and the danger of it. He held that in the pulpit it is "less a crime to cause a momentary laughter than a half-hour's profound slumber,"[19] yet his sermons were very far from being a stream of humor. This could sometimes be a challenge for him, as he once confessed to a listener who objected to some pulpit witticism of his: "If you had known how many others I kept back, you would not have found fault with that one, but you would have commended me for the restraint I had exercised."[20] "Were I not watchful, I should become too hilarious."[21] Yet, he explained, "God's servants have no right to become mere entertainers of the public pouring out a number of stale jokes and idle tales without a practical point. . . . To make religious teaching interesting is one thing, but to make silly mirth, without aim or purpose is quite another."[22]

For all that, it would be wholly inadequate and superficial simply to think of Spurgeon as chucklesome. Humor, he believed, is normally the fruit of something deeper. Sometimes it can come from no more than high spirits—and this, he admitted, *was* a temperamental challenge for him.

> We must—some of us especially must—*conquer our tendency to levity.* A great distinction exists between holy cheerfulness, which is a virtue, and that general levity, which is a vice. There is a levity which has not enough heart to laugh, but trifles with everything; it is flippant, hollow, unreal.[23]

At other times humor can be the defense mechanism of the sad, a light thrown out into the darkness. Sometimes it is the cruel weapon of the

---

18 Williams, *Personal Reminiscences of Charles Haddon Spurgeon*, 77–78.
19 *Autobiog.*, 2:155.
20 *Autobiog.*, 3:346.
21 *ARM*, 394–95.
22 *S&T: 1879*, 133–34.
23 *ARM*, 46.

proud or insecure, brandished as a sneer or a sarcastic put-down.[24] Sometimes it is the bright weapon of righteousness, lancing both gloom and sin.

> I do believe in my heart that there may be as much holiness in a laugh as
> in a cry; and that, sometimes, to laugh is the better thing of the two, for
> I may weep, and be murmuring, and repining, and thinking all sorts of
> bitter thoughts against God; while, at another time, I may laugh the laugh
> of sarcasm against sin, and so evince a holy earnestness in the defence
> of the truth. I do not know why ridicule is to be given up to Satan as a
> weapon to be used against us, and not to be employed by us as a weapon
> against him. I will venture to affirm that the Reformation owed almost as
> much to the sense of the ridiculous in human nature as to anything else,
> and that those humorous squibs and caricatures, that were issued by the
> friends of Luther, did more to open the eyes of Germany to the abomina-
> tions of the priesthood than the more solid and ponderous arguments
> against Romanism.[25]

Most essentially, though, Spurgeon's sunny manner was a manifestation of that happiness and cheer which is found in Christ, the light of the
world. The "levity" he found in himself, and questioned, was inextricably
related to his clear refusal to take himself—or any other sinner—too seriously. Spurgeon held that to be alive in Christ means to fight not only the
habits and acts of sin but also sin's temperamental sullenness, ingratitude,
bitterness, and despair. To enter into Christ's life entails entering into the
joy of being fully human, at peace with the "blessed" or "happy" God of
glory (1 Tim. 1:11):

> Man was not originally made to mourn; he was made to rejoice. The garden
> of Eden was his place of happy abode; and, so long as he continued obedi-
> ent to God, nothing grew in that garden which could cause him sorrow.
> For his delight, the flowers breathed out their perfume. For his delight, the
> landscapes were full of beauty, and the rivers rippled over golden sands.
> God made human beings, as he made his other creatures, to be happy. They
> are capable of happiness, they are in their right element when they are
> happy; and now that Jesus Christ has come to restore the ruins of the Fall,
> he has come to bring back to us the old joy,—only it shall be even sweeter
> and deeper than it could have been if we had never lost it. A Christian has

---

24 *ARM*, 272–73.
25 *Lectures*, 3:43–44.

never fully realized what Christ came to make him until he has grasped the joy of the Lord. Christ wishes his people to be happy. When they are perfect, as he will make them in due time, they shall also be perfectly happy. As heaven is the place of pure holiness, so is it the place of unalloyed happiness; and in proportion as we get ready for heaven, we shall have some of the joy which belongs to heaven, and it is our Saviour's will that even now his joy should remain in us, and that our joy should be full.[26]

Since he saw that Christ wishes his people to be happy, happiness was a vital component of the Christian life for him, and one he sought to possess and display. Indeed, he felt, only when Christ's joy is in us can we be said to be truly Christlike (John 15:11), and only then will we mirror his own attractive appeal.

It is a very vulgar error to suppose that a melancholy countenance is the index of a gracious heart. I commend cheerfulness to all who would win souls; not levity and frothiness, but a genial, happy spirit. There are more flies caught with honey than with vinegar, and there will be more souls led to heaven by a man who wears heaven in his face than by one who bears Tartarus in his looks.[27]

Living as a Child of the Creator

There was one way in which Spurgeon was less than full of life: naturally unathletic, he was prone from childhood to be physically timid and unadventurous. That said, his view of the Christian life gave him a boldness quite unnatural to his constitution. He saw that in Christ he was adopted and loved by an omnipotent Father who reigns, sovereign over all things. It meant that everything fearful—all opposition and danger—tended to shrink in his sight. When rightly viewed, nothing could cause despair, for everything exists under the almighty hand of God the Father, ruler on high. Where, for example, others (like the unregenerate young Martin Luther) might be terrified at lightning, Spurgeon declared, "I love the lightnings, God's thunder is my delight":

Men are by nature afraid of the heavens; the superstitious dread the signs in the sky, and even the bravest spirit is sometimes made to tremble when

---

[26] *MTP*, 51:229.
[27] *Lectures*, 1:184. "Tartarus" is the gloomy abyss of punishment mentioned in 2 Pet. 2:4.

the firmament is ablaze with lightning, and the pealing thunder seems
to make the vast concave of heaven to tremble and to reverberate; but I
always feel ashamed to keep indoors when the thunder shakes the solid
earth, and the lightnings flash like arrows from the sky. Then God is
abroad, and I love to walk out in some wide space, and to look up and
mark the opening gates of heaven, as the lightning reveals far beyond, and
enables me to gaze into the unseen. I like to hear my Heavenly Father's
voice in the thunder.[28]

What was there for him to fear in all the awesome forces of a storm? All
were merely the tools and expressions of his perfect and loving heavenly
Father.

And seeing that *all* things are the Father's and have their being from
him also gave Spurgeon a broad interest in his Father's creation. Brought up
in the countryside, under the broad skies of East Anglia, he loved spending
time outside, often in his garden, enjoying trees, flowers, birds, rainbows,
and all the rich variety of creation. He was also curious, and read exten-
sively on horticulture and biology, the knowledge and enjoyment of which
leaked through into so much of his teaching. And often even his brief re-
marks reveal how keen was his interest in botany:

You know that in the habit of opening and closing, flowers are so varied
that some one or other of them is sure to be opening at each quarter of an
hour of the day. The star of Jerusalem is up by three, and the chicory at
four: the buttercup opens at six, the water-lily at seven, the pink at eight,
and so on till the night comes on. Linnæus made a clock of flowers. If you
are well acquainted with the science of botany, you, too, may tell the time
without a watch.[29]

Rather like Jonathan Edwards, Spurgeon believed that it is right to
"read" creation as a book full of testimony to the Creator and his ways. In
one article in his church's magazine, *The Sword and the Trowel*, he wrote of
the church as "the Garden of God," in which different sorts of believers are
like different flowers. Some bright and cheerful Christians seem to live their
lives "on a warm border where no biting wind ever makes its way." They are
like the spring crocus, bathing and flourishing and rejoicing in the sunlight.

[28] *Autobiog.*, 1:205.
[29] *S&T: 1882*, 139.

See the crocus fast closed while "the clouds return after the rain," but open and filled with glory when the sun pours its rays into its cup of pure gold like unto transparent glass. At such times did you ever note the soft golden flame which seems to burn deep down in the cup,—a sort of fiery sheen of liquid light? How like to the raptures and ecstasies which are enjoyed by certain of our Lord's household! A clear, warm, steady sunshine is the element of the crocus; under such influence it throws out a blaze of colour.[30]

Others seem inclined to the shady side of life, and can be likened to the evening primrose. This patient flower looks quite faded and drab next to the crocus in the full sunlight, but wait until twilight,

and you shall see it gradually open its fragrant blossoms, and display its pale yellow colours. It is the joy of the evening and the night: the garish sun woos it in vain, it loves the fair face of the moon. We all know godly women who would never be seen to advantage among the public activities of our churches, and yet in the sick-room and in the hour of affliction they are full of beauty, and shed a lovely fragrance all around.[31]

The lesson Spurgeon draws is that God has so ordered his creation and his church as to make everything beautiful in its season. There should be no conflict among either saints or flowers over which is better: the Creator has arranged them all deliberately for different times, seasons, and soils. One flower, however, every Christian should seek to emulate: the marguerite, which shuts itself up to the darkness and only unfurls its petals to welcome the sun.

Should we not act according to such sort towards the Well-beloved, whose presence makes our day? When our Lord Christ conceals his face, let us shut up our hearts in sorrow, even "as the closing buds at eve grieve for the departed sunbeams." When Jesus shines upon us with brightness of beauty and warmth of grace, then let our hearts unclasp their folded leaves again, and let them drink in a fulness of light and love.[32]

It was not just botany that appealed to Spurgeon; his intellectual curiosity was deliberately all-encompassing. He held that it is foolish, de-

[30] *S&T: 1882*, 137–38.
[31] *S&T: 1882*, 138.
[32] *S&T: 1882*, 139.

humanizing, and therefore unchristian for Christians to confine themselves to thinking only about overtly "spiritual" matters. We live in this
fallen world on a "war-footing," to be sure, dedicating ourselves to spreading the gospel of Christ among the nations. However, the Father has made—
and is therefore concerned with—all things; moreover, he has made the
world for mankind to rule over. It would be both ungodlike and a simple
dereliction of duty for us to shut our minds to those things on earth that
occupy his.[33] We must, therefore, neglect no field of knowledge.

> The presence of Jesus on the earth has sanctified the whole realm of na-
> ture; and what He has cleansed, call not you common. All that your Father
> has made is yours, and you should learn from it. You may read a natural-
> ist's journal, or a traveller's narrative of his voyages, and find profit in it.
> Yes, and even an old herbal, or a manual of alchemy may, like Samson's
> dead lion, yield you honey. There are pearls in oyster shells, and sweet
> fruits on thorny boughs. The paths of true science, especially natural his-
> tory and botany, drop fatness. Geology, so far as it is fact, and not fiction,
> is full of treasures. History—wonderful are the visions which it makes to
> pass before you,—is eminently instructive; indeed, every portion of God's
> dominion in nature teems with precious teachings.[34]

More than that, Christ is the logic and the light of the world; the gospel
is the sum of all wisdom; the Scriptures are able to make us wise—and
not just for salvation. Christians should therefore be wise and omnivorous
people of comprehensive intellect.

> A man who is a believing admirer and a hearty lover of the truth, as it is
> in Jesus, is in a right place to follow with advantage any other branch of
> science. . . . Once when I read books, I put all my knowledge together in
> glorious confusion; but ever since I have known Christ, I have put Christ
> in the centre as my sun, and each science revolves round it like a planet,
> while minor sciences are satellites to these planets.[35]

Like us all, Spurgeon was uniquely himself. Yet his big-heartedness
and joy as he walked through his Father's creation displays exactly the sort
of life that will always grow from the theology he believed.

---

[33] ARM, 35.
[34] ARM, 36–37.
[35] NPSP, 1:60.

PART 2

CHRIST THE CENTER

CHAPTER 2

CHRIST AND THE BIBLE

Spurgeon once remarked to his students that the mighty fourth- and fifth-century preacher John "Chrysostom" ("Golden Mouth") was so-called because "he had learned his Bible by heart, so as to be able to repeat it at his pleasure."[1] Spurgeon would no doubt have attributed his own power as a preacher to the same cause, for he himself was a man full of Scripture. Words he famously used to describe his beloved John Bunyan apply equally well to him:

> It is blessed to eat into the very soul of the Bible until, at last, you come to talk in Scriptural language, and your very style is fashioned upon Scripture models, and, what is better still, your spirit is flavoured with the words of the Lord. I would quote John Bunyan as an instance of what I mean. Read anything of his, and you will see that it is almost like reading the Bible itself. He . . . cannot give us his *Pilgrim's Progress*—that sweetest of all prose poems,—without continually making us feel and say, "Why, this man is a living Bible!" Prick him anywhere; and you will find that his blood is Bibline, the very essence of the Bible flows from him. He cannot speak without quoting a text, for his soul is full of the Word of God.[2]

You can pick almost any sermon—and most of his letters—to prove the point: scriptural images, idioms, and references crowd Spurgeon's every paragraph and seemed to spill out of him in an entirely natural and unforced way.

---

[1] *Lectures*, 1:71.
[2] *Autobiog.*, 4:268.

It was really the natural consequence of having the highest and warmest view of the Bible. "Inerrancy" was not a term in use in Spurgeon's day, though undoubtedly he held to what today would be called an inerrantist view of Scripture. He repeatedly taught, defended, and dedicated whole sermons to what he called the "infallibility" of Scripture.[3] One of his first sermons in London as the pastor of New Park Street Chapel was on the subject of the Bible; in it he articulated the classic view of infallibility (or inerrancy, as it would be called today):

> Here lies my Bible—who wrote it? I open it, and I find it consists of a series of tracts. The first five tracts were written by a man called Moses. I turn on and I find others. Sometimes I see David is the penman, at other times, Solomon. Here I read Micah, then Amos, then Hosea. As I turn further on, to the more luminous pages of the New Testament, I see Matthew, Mark, Luke, and John, Paul, Peter, James and others; but when I shut up the book, I ask myself who is the author of it? Do these men jointly claim the authorship? Are they the compositors of this massive volume? Do they between themselves divide the honour? Our holy religion answers, No! This volume is the writing of the living God: each letter was penned with an Almighty finger; each word in it dropped from the everlasting lips, each sentence was dictated by the Holy Spirit. Albeit, that Moses was employed to write his histories with his fiery pen, God guided that pen.[4]

That is, God is the trustworthy divine author of every letter of Scripture; God uses human authors to convey (in many different styles and genres) what he means to say. It needs to be said that when Spurgeon spoke like this of the absolute and total trustworthiness of Scripture, he was referring to the original manuscripts and not to any translation. He believed that the Authorized or King James Version was perhaps unsurpassable as a translation, and yet he could say, "I sometimes am ashamed of this translation . . . when I see how, in some important points, it is not true to God's Word."[5]

Furthermore, he saw that since the Bible is God's own Word, it is both supreme and foundational in its authority. All other authorities must bow to it, and no authority—no church, scholar, or pope—need sit behind or

---

[3] See, for example, sermon 2013 in *MTP*, 34:145–56.

[4] *NPSP*, 1:110. Spurgeon was keen not to indulge in what he felt would be speculation concerning the mechanics of the inspiration of Scripture. However, it would be inaccurate to take from these words that he held to a mechanical-dictation theory: while God "guided that pen," it was Moses who wrote. The human authorship of the Scriptures was also important to Spurgeon, as can be seen clearly in his *Treasury of David*, where he considers the Psalms as the songs *of the saints*.

[5] *NPSP*, 4:59.

above it, offering some otherwise lacking endorsement. The Bible, in other words, is self-attesting in its supremacy.

> There is a peculiar majesty, a remarkable fulness, a singular potency, a divine sweetness, in any word of God, which is not discoverable, nor anything like it, in the word of man. . . . It is God's inspired teaching, infallible, and infinitely pure. We accept it as the very word of the living God, every jot and tittle of it, not so much because there are external evidences which go to show its authenticity,—a great many of us do not know anything about those evidences, and probably never shall,—but because we discern an inward evidence in the words themselves. They have come to us with a power that no other words ever had in them, and we cannot be argued out of our conviction of their superlative excellence and divine authority.[6]

Christ and His Word

For all his reverence for the Scriptures and his supremely high view of them, Spurgeon was no bibliolater. That was because he thought of the Bible not as an object in its own right to be considered independently but as "the word *of Christ*" (Rom. 10:17; Col. 3:16). Thus his regard for the Bible was one with his regard for Christ. For him, the Bible was no rival to Christ but the Word and revelation of Christ through which Christ is received and his will made known. To suggest that the Bible might be fallible would be to suggest that Christ is a fallible teacher. Indifference to the Bible would be indifference to him. "How can we reverence His person, if His own words and those of His apostles are treated with disrespect? Unless we receive Christ's words, we cannot receive Christ."[7]

Spurgeon expanded on this theme in a sermon he preached in 1888, "The Word a Sword." His text was Hebrews 4:12, "For the word of God is living and active, sharper than any two-edged sword." In seeking to understand the verse, he found himself torn between the interpretative camps of John Calvin and John Owen. On the one hand, Calvin (among many others) took "the word of God" there to refer to *the Bible*; on the other, Owen and others had understood it as denoting *Christ*, the eternal Word. Spurgeon felt that the very existence of the difficulty—with two such eminent and careful exegetes disagreeing as to which was meant—was itself instructive.

---

[6] *MTP*, 18:618–19.
[7] *ARM*, 373.

This shows us a great truth, which we might not otherwise have so clearly noted. How much that can be said of the Lord Jesus may be also said of the inspired volume! How closely are these two allied! How certainly do those who despise the one reject the other! How intimately are the Word made flesh, and the Word uttered by inspired men, joined together![8]

The book *is* the revelation of Christ, who is the eternal Word and revelation of his Father; as such, it cannot be considered apart from Christ. The book is living and active *because* Christ is living and active. And just as Christ cannot be left out of Scripture, so Scripture cannot be apart from Christ. "Take thou this Book, and distil it into one word, and that one word will be Jesus. The Book itself is but the body of Christ, and we may look upon all its pages as the swaddling bands of the infant Saviour; for if we unroll the Scripture, we come upon Jesus Christ himself."[9]

The inseparability of the Bible from Christ meant that Spurgeon held no abstract doctrine of infallibility/inerrancy for the sake of a culturally innate Enlightenment rationalism. He treasured the Bible and held it to be entirely trustworthy because he treasured Christ and held him to be entirely trustworthy. (And, sealing the bond between the two, he treasured Christ because the Bible self-evidently presents him as self-evidently good, beautiful, and true.)

It also meant that Spurgeon could only be interested in the Christ of the Bible, unlike those who love a "Jesus" other than the one made known in Scripture.

There are some nowadays who deny every doctrine of revelation, and yet, forsooth, they praise the Christ. The Teacher is spoken of in the most flattering style, and then his teaching is rejected, except so far as it may coincide with the philosophy of the moment. They talk much about Jesus, while that which is the real Jesus, namely, his gospel, and his inspired Word, they cast away. I believe I do but correctly describe them when I say that, like Judas, they betray the Son of man with a kiss.[10]

Scripture's Great Theme

The fact that Scripture is the Word of Christ, that its purpose and main theme is Christ, served as a strong melodic line throughout Spurgeon's

---

[8] *MTP*, 34:109.
[9] "How to Become Full of Joy," in *MTP*, 57:496.
[10] *MTP*, 34:110.

thought and ministry. By "Scripture" here, we need to be clear that Spurgeon meant *both* the Old and New Testaments: from beginning to end, Scripture is the Word of and about Christ. "We may begin at Genesis and go on to the Book of Revelation, and say of all the holy histories, 'These are written that ye might believe that Jesus is the Christ, the Son of God.'"[11]

This meant that when his congregation sat to hear him expound an Old Testament passage, they could be quite sure they would hear an explicitly *Christian* sermon. And it was not just that the prophets prophesied Christ's future comings and that the many types found in the Law and the histories (prophets, priests, kings, saviors, sacrifices, etc.) described what he would come to be and do. As Spurgeon saw it, the Old Testament did point forward to Christ in those ways—but it did more than that. Old Testament believers would be described as fellow brothers and sisters of the same faith, as friends of Christ. Spurgeon could speak this way because he was insistent and clear that there is no creator or covenant Lord other than Christ, the eternal Son of the Father. Not only was Christ prophesied in the Old Testament; he was actively present in it.

He was the divine Word through whom his Father brought all things into being; he was the one who conversed with Adam and Eve in Eden. "It was Jesus who walked in the garden of Eden in the cool of the day, for his delights were with the sons of men."[12]

> Time rolled on, and men fell, and afterwards multiplied upon the face of the earth; but Christ's delights were still with the sons of men, and often did he, in one form or another, visit this earth, to converse with Abraham, or to wrestle with Jacob, or to speak with Joshua, or to walk in the burning fiery furnace with Shadrach, Meshach, and Abed-nego. He was always anticipating the time when he should actually assume human nature, and fulfil his covenant engagements.[13]

Spurgeon taught that it was Jesus who led his people out of Egypt (Jude 5), who met and communed with Moses in the burning bush and with Solomon and Ezekiel in their visions, who told Isaac, "Fear not, I am with you."[14] Especially the divine Son would visit the faithful, like Abraham: "Friends are sure to visit one another."[15]

---

[11] *MTP*, 27:654.
[12] *NPSP*, 2:31.
[13] *MTP*, 47:361.
[14] *MTP*, 27:38; 45:600; 26:229; 27:37–44; 35:25–36.
[15] *MTP*, 33:269.

The Sun among Doctrines

Spurgeon's view of the Bible found its purpose and place in the light of Christ. In fact, in his mind, all doctrines found their proper place only in their orbit around Christ. (For this reason, an exemplary introduction to Spurgeon's thought and preaching is *Christ's Glorious Achievements*.)[16] In this way, Spurgeon saw theology much like astronomy: as the solar system makes sense only when the sun is central, so systems of theological thought are coherent only when Christ is central. Every doctrine must find its place and meaning in its proper relation to Christ. "Be assured that we cannot be right in the rest, unless we think rightly of HIM. . . . Where is Christ in your theological system?"[17] Thus when, for example, we think about the doctrine of election, we must remember that we are elect *in Christ*; when we think of adoption, we must remember we are adopted only *in him*. And on and on: we are justified in him, preserved in him, perfected, raised, and glorified in him. Every blessing of the gospel is found in him, "for he is all the best things in one."[18]

Yet even that astronomical analogy may be too weak to capture quite how Christ-centered Spurgeon was in his thinking. For him, Christ is not merely one component—however pivotal—in the bigger machinery of the gospel. Christ is not the peddler of some truth, reward, or message other than himself, as if *through* Christ we get the *real* deal, whether that be heaven, grace, life, or whatever. "It is Christ, and not heaven, the dying need. He who receives Christ gets heaven. He who has no Christ would be miserable in paradise."[19] Christ himself *is* the truth we know, the object and reward of our faith, and the light that illumines every part of a true theological system. In the ground-setting preface to his first volume of sermons he wrote:

> Jesus is *the Truth*. We believe *in him*,—not merely in his words. *He* himself is Doctor and Doctrine, Revealer and Revelation, the Illuminator and the Light of Men. He is exalted in every word of truth, because he is its sum and substance. He sits above the gospel, like a prince on his own throne. Doctrine is most precious when we see it distilling from his lips and embodied in his person. Sermons are valuable in proportion as they speak

16 C. H. Spurgeon, *Christ's Glorious Achievements* (Edinburgh and Carlisle, PA: Banner of Truth, 2014).
17 *ARM*, 364.
18 *NPSP*, 5:141.
19 *S&T: 1881*, 194.

of him and point *to* him. A Christless gospel is no gospel and a Christless discourse is the cause of merriment to devils.[20]

Christ being the glory of God, he lightens every doctrine, and it is only in his radiance that Christian doctrines are and show themselves to be glorious. That is why, Spurgeon wrote, "You cannot taste the sweetness of any *doctrine* till you have remembered Christ's connection with it."[21] It also helps to explain Spurgeon's passion for biblical orthodoxy, seen most clearly in the bitter fight of the "Down Grade Controversy."[22] It was not that he had an inflexible attachment to some abstract system of thought; liberalism and false teaching he saw as a direct assault upon the very nature and glory of the Christ who died for him. Note, then, how immediately he moves here from "the gospel" to the Savior: "My blood boils with indignation at the idea of improving the gospel. There is but one Savior, and that one Savior is the same for ever."[23]

With such a strong gravitational pull to Christ in his theology, it could be thought that Spurgeon had succumbed to a skewed Christomonism. That was never the case, though: recognizing Christ as the Spirit-anointed Son and glory of his Father, Spurgeon's Christ-centeredness was Trinitarian all through. Thus, in preaching or writing on *Christ*, he would often be drawn into rich and thoughtful Trinitarian mediations, as witnesses the opening material of his very first sermon as pastor of New Park Street Chapel:

> The most excellent study for expanding the soul, is the science of Christ, and him crucified, and the knowledge of the Godhead in the glorious Trinity. Nothing will so enlarge the intellect, nothing so magnify the whole soul of man, as a devout, earnest, continued investigation of the great subject of the Deity. And, whilst humbling and expanding, this subject is eminently *consolatary*. Oh, there is, in contemplating Christ, a balm for every wound; in musing on the Father, there is a quietus for every grief; and in the influence of the Holy Ghost, there is a balsam for every sore. Would you lose your sorrows? Would you drown your cares? Then go, plunge yourself in the Godhead's deepest sea; be lost in his immensity; and you shall come forth as from a couch of rest, refreshed and

---

[20] *NPSP*, 1:vi.
[21] *S&T: 1865*, 7.
[22] See "The Down Grade," in *S&T: 1887*, 122.
[23] *MTP*, 34:80.

invigorated. I know nothing which can so comfort the soul; so calm the swelling billows of grief and sorrow; so speak peace to the winds of trial, as a devout musing upon the subject of the Godhead.[24]

How to Read the Bible

In 1879, Spurgeon preached a sermon titled "How to Read the Bible," which summed up his experiential, Christ-centered approach to Scripture.

His first point was that to read the Bible properly, the reader must *understand* what is written. "Understanding the meaning is the essence of true reading."[25] From the start Spurgeon is clear that in seeking to be experiential, he will not allow the sort of mysticism that bypasses the intellect. It is *"the light of the knowledge* of the glory of God in the face of Jesus Christ" (2 Cor. 4:6) that transforms us "into the same image from one degree of glory to another" (2 Cor. 3:18). "There must be knowledge of God before there can be love to God: there must be a knowledge of divine things, as they are revealed, before there can be an enjoyment of them."[26]

Much, then, that passes for Bible reading is really no Bible reading at all, as Spurgeon understood it. "Do not many of you read the Bible in a very hurried way—just a little bit, and off you go?" he asked. "How few of you are resolved to get at its soul, its juice, its life, its essence, and to drink in its meaning."[27] When the eye freewheels over verses and leaves the mind unengaged, that is no true reading. It is much more likely to be evidence of the crude superstition that religion demands an unthinking performance of a regular reading ritual. Where others go on pilgrimages and perform penances, evangelicals throw their eyes over chapters of the Bible—and could do it just as well with the book turned upside down. Indeed, Spurgeon would drive home this point deeper, arguing that the mind must be more than listlessly engaged:

> Reading has a kernel to it, and the mere shell is little worth. In prayer there is such a thing as praying in prayer—a praying that is the bowels of the prayer. So in praise there is a praising in song, an inward fire of intense devotion which is the life of the hallelujah. It is so in fasting: there

---

[24] *NPSP*, 1:1.
[25] *MTP*, 25:627.
[26] *MTP*, 25:627.
[27] *MTP*, 25:631.

is a fasting which is not fasting, and there is an inward fasting, a fasting of the soul, which is the soul of fasting. It is even so with the reading of the Scriptures. There is an interior reading, a kernel reading—a true and living reading of the Word. This is the soul of reading; and, if it be not there, the reading is a mechanical exercise, and profits nothing.[28]

True Bible reading thus requires wakeful, attentive study and deep reflection on what is written. That is just why, in his clear and luminous Word, God has put so many challenging and obscure passages, that our appetite for divine things might be whetted and our minds compelled to be active. "Meditation and careful thought exercise us and strengthen the soul for the reception of the yet more lofty truths. . . . We must meditate, brothers. These grapes will yield no wine till we tread upon them."[29]

Such fully engaged reading of Scripture must involve prayer. "It is a grand thing to be driven to think, it is a grander thing to be driven to pray through having been made to think."[30] After all, Scripture is the Spirit-breathed Word of God: we read it to know him, and we need his help. Such reading must also be ready to seek help toward deeper understanding.

> Some, under the pretence of being taught of the Spirit of God refuse to be instructed by books or by living men. This is no honouring of the Spirit of God; it is a disrespect to him, for if he gives to some of his servants more light than to others—and it is clear he does—then they are bound to give that light to others, and to use it for the good of the church.[31]

Spurgeon's second main point was that in reading we should seek out Scripture's *meaning* and *intent*. Beyond simple understanding, this involves finding spiritual *instruction*. Reading a historical passage, for example about Moses's bronze snake (Numbers 21), we learn *more* than history: we learn about the nature of living faith. Reading a passage from the Law, for example about the tabernacle (Exodus 25–31), we learn about the nature of God's holiness and atonement. Reading a passage filled with explicit doctrine, we seek not simply to comprehend it but

[28] *MTP*, 25:627.
[29] *MTP*, 25:629.
[30] *MTP*, 25:629.
[31] *MTP*, 25:630.

to be affected and altered by it. More than understanding, such reading involves transformation.

> I have sorrowfully observed some persons who are very orthodox, and who can repeat their creed very glibly, and yet the principal use that they make of their orthodoxy is to sit and watch the preacher with the view of framing a charge against him. . . . [They] know nothing about the things of God in their real meaning. They have never drank them into their souls, but only sucked them up into their mouths to spit them out on others. . . . Therefore, beloved, never be satisfied with a sound creed, but desire to have it graven on the tablets of your heart.[32]

At its root, the transformation Spurgeon desired for readers of the Bible was a turning away from the sin that deadens and to the Christ who makes alive. Scripture draws us to enjoy a living communion with Jesus, and that is what he would call "the soul of Scripture." "If you do not find Jesus in the Scriptures they will be of small service to you, for what did our Lord himself say? 'Ye search the Scriptures, for in them ye think ye have eternal life, but *ye will not come unto me* that ye might have life.'"[33] Thus he urged on those who would read the Bible this experiential, Trinitarian, Christ-centered prayer:

> O living Christ, make this a living word to me. Thy word is life, but not without the Holy Spirit. I may know this book of thine from beginning to end, and repeat it all from Genesis to Revelation, and yet it may be a dead book, and I may be a dead soul. But, Lord, be present here; then will I look up from the book to the Lord; from the precept to him who fulfilled it; from the law to him who honoured it; from the threatening to him who has borne it for me, and from the promise to him in whom it is "Yea and amen."[34]

His third and last point was really a simple encouragement: Scripture reading is *profitable*. It is worth all the investment of time and of mental and emotional energy. That is because it is the Spirit's means of imparting new life. "We are begotten by the word of God: it is the instrumental means

---

32 *MTP*, 25:633.
33 *MTP*, 25:634–35. Elsewhere he argued, "*Holy Scripture was not written with the mere view of imparting knowledge to men by presenting them with a complete biography of Jesus Christ.* The one intent of Scripture is that ye may believe on Jesus Christ" (*MTP*, 27:656).
34 *MTP*, 25:633–34.

of regeneration. Therefore love your Bibles. Keep close to your Bibles."[35] We are initially regenerated and we are continually vitalized by the light of the knowledge of the glory of God in the face of Jesus Christ held out to us in Scripture. So, "cling you to Scripture. Scripture is not Christ, but it is the silken clue which will lead you to him."[36]

"It will lead you to him." That was the point of the Bible, as Spurgeon saw it. Indeed, it was the point of all his theology.

---

[35] *MTP*, 25:635.
[36] *MTP*, 25:635.

CHAPTER 3

PURITANISM, CALVINISM, AND CHRIST

Charles Spurgeon has often been accorded the title *Ultimus Puritanorum* ("the last of the Puritans"). He himself rejected it for the simple reason that he spent much of his energy educating and training pastors who might carry on the Puritan tradition. "The doctrine which I preach is that of the Puritans."[1] Indeed, he once boasted, "I have been charged with being a mere echo of the Puritans."[2] He was, in other words, a self-conscious, card-carrying Puritan, but he refused to be the last of that line. Like most sixteenth- and seventeenth-century Puritans, he was also unambiguously and unashamedly Calvinist.

For Spurgeon to have held such theology in nineteenth-century Britain was, frankly, remarkable. The rise of theological liberalism and Anglo-Catholicism in his day tended to make Calvinistic Puritanism look quaintly olde worlde and not a little pea-brained. More remarkable still was the unbigoted way in which he held this theology. Being so out of step with the theological climate of his day could easily have made him prickly and clannish, yet for all his unbending theological resolution, Spurgeon was strikingly broad-minded. And it is not hard to see why: Spurgeon was a Puritan and a Calvinist not through adherence to any theological system or tradition as such but because he believed such theology most glorifies Christ.

---

[1] *Autobiog.*, 2:87.
[2] *ARM*, 10. See also Ernest W. Bacon, *Spurgeon: Heir of the Puritans* (London: George Allen & Unwin, 1967).

Born and Bred a Puritan

The village of Stambourne, Essex, where Spurgeon spent his formative childhood years, is in the heart of what was once England's Puritan country. The independent congregation there was founded when the Puritan rector Henry Havers was ejected from the Church of England in 1662. There, in what had been Havers's manse, Spurgeon was raised by his grandfather, a gifted preacher who strongly maintained the Calvinistic and Puritan legacy of the chapel. The influence of the Puritans could clearly be felt in the family's devotions together, and it was quite normal for the adults to read passages from Puritan writings to the children. Spurgeon once explicitly mentioned in a sermon how on Sunday evenings his mother would read to them from Joseph Alleine's *Alarm to the Unconverted* and Richard Baxter's *Call to the Unconverted*.[3]

Perhaps as influential as any of these things was the presence of Havers's old study, upstairs in the manse. The windows had been filled in since his day, leaving it a dark but private place. There the young Spurgeon would retreat, and there he got to rummage through a library of Puritan works.

> Some of these were enormous folios, such as a boy could hardly lift. Here I first struck up acquaintance with the martyrs, and specially with "Old Bonner," who burned them; next, with Bunyan and his "Pilgrim"; and further on, with the great masters of Scriptural theology, with whom no moderns are worthy to be named in the same day. Even the old editions of their works, with their margins and old-fashioned notes, are precious to me. It is easy to tell a real Puritan book even by its shape and by the appearance of the type. I confess that I harbour a prejudice against nearly all new editions, and cultivate a preference for the originals, even though they wander about in sheepskins and goatskins, or are shut up in the hardest of boards. It made my eyes water, a short time ago, to see a number of these old books in the new Manse: I wonder whether some other boy will love them, and live to revive that grand old divinity which will yet be to England her balm and benison.[4]

For the rest of his life, Spurgeon was an avid and quite omnivorous reader, and would amass a personal library consisting of over twelve thousand

---

[3] *MTP*, 10:418.
[4] *Autobiog.*, 1:22–23.

Figure 1

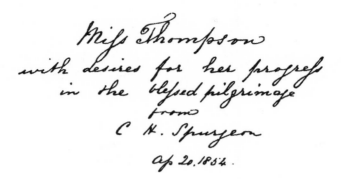

volumes, including what was probably in his day the most extensive private library of Puritan literature anywhere. He would become intimately familiar with all the main Puritan authors, able to detect their different characteristics and styles and to quote many of them from memory.

Without a doubt, his favorite Puritan was the one he called "my old friend John Bunyan,"[5] and his favorite book, Bunyan's *Pilgrim's Progress*. "Next to the Bible, the book that I value most is John Bunyan's 'Pilgrim's Progress.'"[6] He read this over a hundred times, seemed to quote it whenever he could, and in 1854 deemed it the most romantic and appropriate gift he could give his soon-to-be fiancée, Susannah Thompson.[7] In the copy he gave her he inscribed the words shown in figure 1.

Describing the Christian life as "the blessed pilgrimage," Spurgeon revealed how deeply Bunyan's allegory had permeated his imagination and theology. As Spurgeon saw it, the life of the believer, following Christ, is a pilgrimage to heaven. And, as Bunyan would also describe it, it is a *Holy War* (for more on this, see chap. 10). Yet even more than all the Bunyan references and imagery in Spurgeon's sermons and writings, Bunyan helped shape the very way Spurgeon spoke and wrote. Spurgeon instinctively disliked the flowery pretentiousness of Latinate words, but it was from Bunyan more than any other that Spurgeon learned the power and the simplicity of plain and homely Anglo-Saxon.

Part of Spurgeon's Puritan heritage was an instinctive anti-Romanism

---

5 *NPSP*, 1:56.
6 C. H. Spurgeon, *Pictures from Pilgrim's Progress: A Commentary on Portions of John Bunyan's Immortal Allegory* (1903; repr., Pasadena, TX: Pilgrim, 1992), 11.
7 *Autobiog.*, 2:6–7.

that most people today find hard to understand, especially in the United States, where the Reformation martyrs are not a part of the nation's own history. Yet Spurgeon was raised on the stirring accounts in Foxe's *Book of Martyrs* of the torture and burnings of his fellow Protestant countrymen, and even before his conversion he felt compelled to write a scalding essay titled "Antichrist and Her Brood; Or, Popery Unmasked."[8] In one early sermon he spoke of Rome as hell's "incarnate representative";[9] in another, titled "War! War! War!," he declaimed:

> We must have no truce, no treaty with Rome. War! war to the knife with her! Peace there cannot be. She cannot have peace with us—we cannot have peace with her. She hates the true Church; and we can only say that the hatred is reciprocated. We would not lay a hand upon her priests; we would not touch a hair of their heads. Let them be free; but their doctrine we would destroy from the face of the earth as the doctrine of devils.[10]

It is important to note this aspect of his theology (strongest in his early years), for it makes his later comments about Roman Catholics preaching Christ all the more remarkable. Spurgeon never deviated from his adherence to Reformation distinctives (Scripture alone, justification by grace alone through faith alone in Christ alone, etc.), nor from his belief that Roman Catholicism was profoundly and dangerously in error on these matters; however, that does not mean that the mature Spurgeon was some unthinking Protestant bigot. Increasingly, as the years went by, his critiques of Rome did not focus, as once they had, on "her dungeons, . . . her inquisitions, [her] power in the state to cut, and mangle, and burn";[11] it was rather that Rome did not truly preach Christ.

Why Spurgeon Loved the Puritans

"There never were better men in the world than the Puritans," Spurgeon once told his congregation.[12] He felt such affection for them that he had a bowling lawn prepared in his garden so that he might share the favorite sport of such Puritans as Thomas Goodwin, John Howe,

8 Spurgeon's College, Heritage Room (A2.06).
9 *NPSP*, 5:139.
10 *NPSP*, 5:204.
11 *NPSP*, 5:139.
12 *NPSP*, 2:134.

Thomas Manton, John Owen, and Oliver Cromwell. When playing he would imagine what must have gone through their minds during their games: the bias of the bowl, for instance, must surely, he felt, have made them think of the bias of the human will.[13] He was emphatic that the purpose of his Pastors' College was to raise up pastors who would be thoroughly "Puritanic."[14]

But why? Why such admiration and fondness for a group of men so generally vilified by history? Of course, there was his upbringing and the fact that they shared his resolute Protestantism. But there was much more, and his heartfelt attachment to the Puritans is deeply revealing of what most moved and motivated him.

First, Spurgeon admired the depth and seriousness of the Puritans as they studied Scripture, God, humanity, and all reality. He held that they tended to be more wise, rounded, and sensible than most modern preachers and theologians because of their "great erudition, unwearied application, deep-felt experience, and unbounded veneration for the authority of the Divine Word."[15]

Second, he set great store by how worshipful and practical Puritan theology was. In Puritan hands, deep and thoughtful theology was never allowed to become a game for the intelligentsia: it fueled worship and it built up the church. This concern he shared with them, for a heartfelt knowledge of the truth—beyond mere intellectual assent to the doctrines of the gospel—entirely shaped his vision for the Pastors' College. The students there, he argued,

> are not to be warped into philosophers, polished into debaters, carved into metaphysicians, fashioned into literati, or even sharpened into critics, they are to be "thoroughly furnished unto every good work." The Scriptures must be their chief class-book, theology their main science, the art of teaching their practical study, and the proclamation and exposition of the gospel their first business. With all knowledge they may intermeddle; but upon the knowledge of Christ crucified they must dwell. Books and parchments should be prized, but prayer and meditation should be supreme. The head should be stored, but the heart also should be fed with heavenly food. The tutors should be men of equal learning and

---

[13] *Autobiog.*, 3:189–90.
[14] *Autobiog.*, 3:149.
[15] *S&T: 1866*, 31–32. Cf. *NPSP*, 3:2.

grace, sound scholars, but much more sound divines, men of culture, but even more decidedly men of God.[16]

This concern for the reformation of human hearts—as well as minds— by the Word of God meant that the Puritans tended to be pastorally wise, warm, and affectionate preachers. They had a deep reverence for the holiness of God, which worked out practically to make them people of studied devotion and prayer, in public and in private.[17] Moreover, because the Puritans sought to see *hearts* won to God, they saw whole *lives* transformed. And for this, Spurgeon loved them.

Third, Spurgeon especially singled out for praise and study those Puritan preachers and authors who made much of Christ. He placed this quotation from Richard Sibbes before the title page of *The Saint and His Savior*, showing how much he valued and approved of the words:

> The special work of our ministry is to lay open Christ, to hold up the tapestry and unfold the mysteries of Christ. Let us labour therefore to be always speaking somewhat about Christ, or tending that way. When we speak of the law, let it drive us to Christ; when of moral duties, let them teach us to walk worthy of Christ. Christ, or something tending to Christ, should be our theme, and mark to aim at.[18]

Why Spurgeon Was a Calvinist

If the Puritans were friends, and Bunyan his dearest, John Calvin was Spurgeon's theological champion. He felt a kinship with theologians of the Reformed tradition and appreciated those who had prepared the way for it (especially Augustine, whose "works were the great mine out of which Calvin dug his mental wealth"),[19] but among all of these influences Calvin was unparalleled.

> Among all those who have been born of women, there has not risen a greater than John Calvin; no age before him ever produced his equal, and no age afterwards has seen his rival. In theology, he stands alone, shining like a bright fixed star, while other leaders and teachers can only circle

---

[16] *S&T: 1875*, 82.
[17] *NPSP*, 2:134–35.
[18] C. H. Spurgeon, *The Saint and His Savior: The Progress of the Soul in the Knowledge of Jesus* (New York: Sheldon, Blakeman & Co., 1858), ii.
[19] *Autobiog.*, 2:375.

round him, at a great distance,—as comets go streaming through space,—with nothing like his glory or his permanence.[20]

The reason for this was, in essence, quite simple: "Calvinism means the placing of the eternal God at the head of all things. I look at everything through its relation to God's glory."[21] God must be central, and considered first. Theological liberalism, Roman Catholicism, and Arminianism all seemed to him to steal glory from God and give it to man. In those systems, Spurgeon judged that human will and choice were played up and considered first, while God's will and choice were sidelined or forgotten.[22] Calvin's theology, in contrast, is the system of doctrine which most clearly magnifies Christ as a Savior and ascribes all the glory to God, and thus best captures the truth we shall sing for eternity as we gather around God's throne and praise him.

That being the case, and God's glory being what it is, Spurgeon argued that Calvinistic theology is that in which Christians will find the greatest joy. Calvinism's deep view of sin and high view of God's grace are not harsh dogmas, except to those who would rather not think of themselves as sinners. They are liberating, joy-giving truths.

> Some seem to think that we poor souls, who are of the Puritanic school, are "cabin'd, cribb'd, confined" by, from which we would gladly escape. They imagine that we have to check every rising aspiration of our nobler selves, so as to preserve the tyranny of a certain iron system. John Calvin is supposed to ride us like a nightmare, and we lead dogs' lives under his lash. Brethren, it is far otherwise. Little do these slanderers know of our happiness and peace. If they feel more joy in preaching than we do, their felicity is great; but, from their tone and style, I should greatly question it. Observers will have noticed that the joyous element has gone out of many pulpits.[23]

All that being said, Spurgeon took it that "Calvinism" is really nothing but a nickname for faithfully preaching Christ and him crucified. ("I have my own ideas, and those I always state boldly!")[24] For, to preach this

---

[20] *Autobiog.*, 2:372.
[21] *ARM*, 337.
[22] "I am frequently told that I ought to examine at length the various new views which are so continually presented. I decline the invitation: I can smell them, and that satisfies me. I perceive in them nothing which glorifies God or magnifies Christ, but much that puffs up human nature, and I protest that the smell is enough for me" (*S&T: 1877*, 81).
[23] *ARM*, 368–69.
[24] *NPSP*, 1:50.

"Calvinism" is really just to preach the gospel: justification by faith, without works; the sovereignty of God; the eternal, all-conquering love of God; the effective redemption of Christ; and the fact that God is powerful to save and keep to the uttermost.

Spurgeon confessed that he (like everyone else) was a natural-born Arminian, without any instinctive taste for—or appreciation of—God's saving grace.[25] The reason he became a Calvinist was his own experience of that grace. At the time he became a Christian, he believed it was all simply up to him, that God received him because he sought God. Only later did the thought strike him that he would never have sought the Lord in the first place if some influence in his mind and heart had not drawn him to do so. He realized he had been led to trust God through being changed.

> Then, in a moment, I saw that God was at the bottom of it all, and that He was the Author of my faith; and so the whole doctrine of grace opened up to me, and from that doctrine I have not departed to this day, and I desire to make this my constant confession, "I ascribe my change wholly to God."[26]

From there he came to believe the doctrine of election, "because I am quite certain that, if God had not chosen me, I should never have chosen Him."[27] Furthermore, he reasoned, God must have elected him and loved him before he was born, and not on the basis of any intrinsic merit, for he saw no reason in himself why God should have looked on him with any special love. Nor did Christ love him and die for him because he believed: Jesus died long before he ever believed. "Our heavenly Father has blessed us with all spiritual blessings according as he hath chosen us in Christ Jesus from before the foundation of the world. The eternal choice is the well-head from which all the springs of mercy flow."[28] And that, he found, was a great comfort: his eternal security—and the salvation of others—rested not on anything in himself but on God's eternal and immutable decree.[29]

As for the doctrine of human sinful depravity, he had no struggles as a

---

[25] *Autobiog.*, 1:168.
[26] *Autobiog.*, 1:168–69.
[27] *Autobiog.*, 1:170.
[28] *MTP*, 16:265.
[29] C. H. Spurgeon, *The Letters of Charles Haddon Spurgeon* (London: Marshall Brothers, 1923), 39.

Christian, because, he said, "I find myself depraved in heart, and have daily proofs that in my flesh there dwelleth no good thing."[30] That being the case, he saw that salvation could only be the result of God's grace.

> If anyone should ask me what I mean by a Calvinist, I should reply, "He is one who says, *Salvation is of the Lord.*" I cannot find in Scripture any other doctrine than this. It is the essence of the Bible. "He *only* is my rock and my salvation." Tell me anything contrary to this truth, and it will be a heresy; tell me a heresy, and I shall find its essence here, that it has departed from this great, this fundamental, this rock-truth, "God is my rock and my salvation." What is the heresy of Rome, but the addition of something to the perfect merits of Jesus Christ,—the bringing in of the works of the flesh, to assist in our justification? And what is the heresy of Arminianism but the addition of something to the work of the Redeemer?[31]

When it came to the atonement, Spurgeon taught that the blood of Christ is, in itself, more than sufficient to cleanse every creature. He is, after all, limitless in his worth. However, God's intent fixes the *application* of Christ's infinitely sufficient blood: his will is to save a multitude for himself. And Spurgeon was clear that the number of the saved will turn out to be a very great multitude, more than anyone can number:

> I believe there will be more in Heaven than in hell. If anyone asks me why I think so, I answer, because Christ, in everything, is to "have the preeminence," and I cannot conceive how He could have the preeminence if there are to be more in the dominions of Satan than in Paradise. Moreover, I have never read that there is to be in hell a great multitude, which no man could number. I rejoice to know that the souls of all infants, as soon as they die, speed their way to Paradise. Think what a multitude there is of them![32]

But God's intent cannot have been to save everyone, else he would be disappointed. Scripture is clear that a terrible number are lost and bound for hell. Christ, then, cannot have died for those who are or will be in hell. To imagine that Christ bore and was punished for the sins of all people and then that some of those people were themselves in hell punished for those

---

[30] *Autobiog.*, 1:171.
[31] *Autobiog.*, 1:172.
[32] *Autobiog.*, 1:174–75.

same sins for which Christ had already atoned "seems to conflict with all my ideas of Divine justice."[33]

Finally, he taught that this Fatherly God of grace could never allow those who had once become his children ever to fall away. Left to ourselves, of course we would fall away, but God keeps his word, and he will not unchild his children for whom Christ died. Even though they go astray, as the best will, still he will view them as his beloved children. He will discipline them for their sin, but he will not stop loving them and calling them his adopted children. He is constant where they are not, and his purposes to bless will not be defeated.

> The Arminian holds the unnatural, cruel, barbarous idea, that a man may be God's child, and then God may unchild him because he does not behave himself. . . . I do not serve the god of the Arminians at all; . . . The god that saith to-day, and denieth to-morrow; that justifieth to-day, and condemns the next; the god that hath children of his own one day, and lets them be the children of the devil the next, is no relation to my God in the least degree. . . . If he hath set his heart upon a man, he will love him to the end. If he hath chosen him, he hath not chosen him for any merit of his own; therefore he will never cast him away for any demerit of his own. . . . But, children of God, you may lay your heads upon the covenant, and say, with Dr. Watts,—
>
>> "Then should the earth's old pillars shake,
>> And all the wheels of nature break,
>> Our steady souls should fear no more
>> Than solid rocks when billows roar."[34]

Magnifying Christ, Not a System

Spurgeon was a Calvinist, but not for the sake of Calvinism as such. He was aware that for some "being a Calvinist" could mean having John Calvin as an ultimate authority (just as for others "being an Arminian" could mean never going beyond Arminius or Wesley). Such "Calvinism" revolted Spurgeon, who wanted to treat God's Word as the only supreme authority, to be followed, whether or not it might agree with Reformed greats such as John Gill or John Calvin.[35]

---

[33] *Autobiog.*, 1:175–76.
[34] *MTP*, 46:308–9.
[35] *NPSP*, 5:133.

Moreover, Spurgeon was actively fearful of human systems of doctrine and how they can subtly distort God's truth: "Angels may, perhaps, be systematic divines; for men it should be enough to follow the word of God, let its teachings wind as they may."[36] Thus, when, for example, he found himself preaching in a Methodist chapel on Romans 10:13 ("everyone who calls on the name of the Lord will be saved"), he deliberately teased them, saying:

> "Dear me! How wonderfully like John Wesley the apostle talked! *Whosoever* shall call! *Whosoever*! Why, that is a Methodist word, is it not?" "Glory! Glory! Hallelujah!" was heard in all parts of the great building. The preacher paused significantly, and proceeded: "Yes, dear brother, but you read the ninth chapter of this epistle, and see how wonderfully like John Calvin he talked—'That the purpose of God according to election might stand.'" There was no "Glory!" Or "Hallelujah!" following this remark, but many a face was lit up with a significant smile. "The fact is," Mr. Spurgeon added, "that the whole of truth is neither here nor there, neither with this system nor that, neither with this man nor that. Be it ours to know that which is Scriptural in all systems, and to receive it."[37]

He rejoiced in warm fellowship with Methodist, Arminian friends, viewing them as fellow brothers and sisters in Christ and "natural allies" in the gospel of free grace against ritualist and rationalist Christianity. And he was quite prepared to use language he knew would infuriate many a Calvinist: "If truth lies in the valley between the two camps, or if it comprehends both, it is well for us to follow it wherever it goes. We have certainly not thrown away the Five Points, but we may have gained other five."[38] Many would accuse him of inconsistency for his warm endorsement of Wesleyan zeal, but there was in fact nothing fickle or incoherent in it. After all, he never thought of himself *first and foremost* as a Calvinist: "I wish to be called nothing but a Christian."[39]

> We believe in the five great points commonly known as Calvinistic; but we do not regard those five points as being barbed shafts which we are to thrust between the ribs of our fellow-Christians. We look upon them as being five great lamps which help to irradiate the cross; or, rather,

---

[36] *S&T: 1868*, 38.
[37] William Williams, *Personal Reminiscences of Charles Haddon Spurgeon* (London: Passmore & Alabaster, 1895), 59–60.
[38] *S&T: 1874*, 36.
[39] *Autobiog.*, 1:176.

five bright emanations springing from the glorious covenant of our Tri-
une God, and illustrating the great doctrine of Jesus crucified. Against
all comers, especially against all lovers of Arminianism, we defend and
maintain pure gospel truth. At the same time, I can make this public dec-
laration, that I am no Antinomian. I belong not to the sect of those who
are afraid to invite the sinner to Christ. I warn him, I invite him, I ex-
hort him. Hence, then, I have contumely on either hand. Inconsistency is
charged against me by some people, as if anything that God commanded
could be inconsistent; I will glory in such inconsistency even to the end.
I bind myself precisely to no form of doctrine. I love those five points
as being the angles of the gospel, but then I love the centre between the
angles better still.[40]

In part, Spurgeon's catholicity reflected a generosity of spirit and a
humanity that preferred to treat people as people rather than theological
specimens. He had a distaste for bigotry and what Philipp Melanchthon
called the *rabies theologorum* that drives theologians, like dogs, to treat
doctrines as bones to bark over.[41] "We are not to be always going about
the world searching out heresies, like terrier dogs sniffing for rats, and to
be always so confident of our own infallibility that we erect ecclesiastical
stakes at which to roast all who differ from us."[42]

Yet, above all, what shaped Spurgeon's theology—and his attitude toward the theology of others—was Christ. The vital essence of the gospel
and all theology, he taught, is "Christ Jesus, who is the sum and substance
of the gospel; who is in himself all theology."[43] More than anything, it
was what other theologies made of Christ that determined his reaction to
them. Quite surprisingly, given his deep antipathy to Roman Catholicism,
he could even show hearty appreciation for a Roman Catholic sermon if
the priest preached Christ. This happened once when he visited a Roman
Catholic church in Brussels, Belgium. There he heard a sermon in which
the priest

> preached the Lord Jesus with all his might. He spoke of the love of Christ,
> so that I, a very poor hand at the French language, could fully understand
> him, and my heart kept beating within me as he told of the beauties of

---

40 *Autobiog.*, 2:328.
41 *Autobiog.*, 4:61.
42 *ARM*, 47.
43 *MTP*, 7:169; cf. 5:140; 23:865.

Christ, and the preciousness of His blood, and of His power to save the chief of sinners. He did not say, "justification by faith," but he did say, "efficacy of the blood," which comes to very much the same thing. He did not tell us we were saved by grace, and not by our works; but he did say that all the works of men were less than nothing when brought into competition with the blood of Christ, and that the blood of Jesus alone could save. True, there were objectionable sentences, as naturally there must be in a discourse delivered under such circumstances; but I could have gone to the preacher, and have said to him, "Brother, you have spoken the truth;" and if I had been handling his text, I must have treated it in the same way that he did, if I could have done it as well.[44]

That priest did preach Christ, but it was Christlessness that was at the heart of Spurgeon's problem with Roman Catholicism. He acknowledged that there were indeed true and saved believers within the walls of the Roman Catholic Church, and that there were light and truth amid all her superstition and false teaching, but he held that Rome itself was essentially empty of Christ. Visiting Turin, he once compared the Roman Catholic Church to the supposed grave clothes of Christ held in the cathedral there. She holds the clothes and reminders of Christ, but he is not there. The symbols of Christ that fill Rome are hollow and empty.[45]

It would be stopping short to say that Spurgeon valued Christ-centered theology. The Christian who is Calvinist for the sake of the system or the tradition would be nominally Christ-centered simply because of the nature of Calvinism. He wanted Christians to have *more* than a formal confession of faith, however orthodox and Christ-centered. For Spurgeon, healthy theology must involve an earnest and warm *affection* for the Christ who stands above and before all.[46] Christ must be central, but he is truly central only when he is supremely adored.

It is love to Christ that is the root of the matter. I am very sorry, my dear brother, if you should hold unsound views on some points; but I love you with all my heart if Jesus is precious to you. I cannot give up believers' baptism; it is none of mine, and, therefore, I cannot give up my Master's word. I am sure that it is Scriptural. I cannot give up the doctrine of election, it seems to me so plainly in the word; but over the head of all

---

[44] *Autobiog.*, 2:364–65.
[45] *ARM*, 7.
[46] *ARM*, 341.

doctrines and ordinances, and over everything, my brother, I embrace thee in my heart if thou believest in Jesus, and if he be precious to thee, for that is the vital point. These are the matters of heart work that mark a Christian—nothing else is so true a test. If you cannot say, "Jesus is precious to me," I do not care to what church you belong, or what creed you are ready to die for, you do not know the truth of God unless the person of Christ is dear to you.[47]

---

[47] *S&T: 1869*, 146.

CHAPTER 4

CHRIST AND PREACHING

In 1850, aged sixteen, Spurgeon was tricked into preaching his first sermon. At that time, a small preaching group based at St. Andrew's Street Chapel in Cambridge was used to supplying preachers for the surrounding villages. Impressed by the recently converted teenager, the leader of the group asked Spurgeon to go to the little village of Teversham the next evening, "for a young man was to preach there who was not much used to services, and very likely would be glad of company."[1] It was a cunning statement that led him to set off the next day, unsuspecting, with the man he assumed would be preaching. Only then, when he wished the man well, did he find out that he himself was the "young man" scheduled to give the sermon. As they walked, he decided he must speak on the sweetness and love of Jesus, and that his text would be 1 Peter 2:7, "Unto you therefore which believe he [Christ] is precious" (KJV). In that urgent moment, his choice of topic and text was all-revealing, and some twenty years later he wrote, "I am sure it contains the marrow of what I have always taught in the pulpit from that day until now."[2]

The Purpose of Preaching

Spurgeon agreed wholly with the aforementioned words of Richard Sibbes, which he placed before the title page of *The Saint and His Savior*: "The special work of our ministry is to lay open Christ, to hold up the tapestry and

[1] *Autobiog.*, 1:200.
[2] *S&T: 1869*, 139.

unfold the mysteries of Christ."[3] And though Spurgeon does not record it, Sibbes would go on to use a courtship image that would be central for Spurgeon's understanding of preaching: "It is the end of our calling to sue for a marriage between Christ and every soul. We are the friends of the bride, to bring the church to him; and the friends of the church, to bring Christ to them."[4] Since Christ's great and eternal purpose—and the very reason for his death—is to win for himself a bride, the preacher's purpose is, as it were, to woo for Christ. Preachers are called to make Christ known in all his goodness, beauty, and truth, that his people might yield themselves to him, delight in him, and be one with him. They are like Abraham's servant in Genesis 24, commissioned to find a bride for his son Isaac. "For as truly as Abraham sent his servant to seek a bride for his son, we are commissioned to search for those who shall be brought into the church, and at length, as the bride of Christ, sit down at the marriage-feast in the glory-land above."[5]

Driven by that understanding of the preacher's task, Spurgeon's preaching was purposeful in a way that went beyond education. "Give us sermons, and save us from essays!"[6] he pleaded with his students training for pastoral ministry. In the pulpit he sought not merely to *inform* his listeners about the Word of God but also to *draw* both believers and unbelievers to Christ. His aim was to see people transformed at the very deepest level, their affections and desires turning away from their naturally cherished sins to Christ. "The object of all true preaching is the heart: we aim at divorcing the heart from sin, and wedding it to Christ. Our ministry has failed, and has not the divine seal set upon it, unless it makes men tremble, makes them sad, and then anon brings them to Christ, and causes them to rejoice."[7]

Spurgeon felt this so strongly that he was often at his most exasperated when thinking of all the aimless, trotted-out sermons that filled so many of the pulpits of England. "I have often wondered why certain sermons were ever preached, what design the preacher had in concocting them."[8] With friendly but smarting mockery he compared these preachers to Chinese knife throwers who could throw their weapons and—against all odds—deliberately miss the assistant standing against the wall. "'Be not afraid,' says

---

[3] C. H. Spurgeon, *The Saint and His Savior: The Progress of the Soul in the Knowledge of Jesus* (New York: Sheldon, Blakeman & Co., 1858), ii.
[4] Richard Sibbes, "Bowels Opened," in *The Complete Works of Richard Sibbes*, ed. A. B. Grosart, 7 vols. (Edinburgh: James Nichol, 1862), 2:142.
[5] *MTP*, 37:589.
[6] *ARM*, 347.
[7] *MTP*, 27:530.
[8] *ARM*, 116.

the preacher, 'I am never personal. I never give home-thrusts.' Stand quite still, my friend! Open your arms! Spread out your fingers! Your minister has practised a very long while, and he knows how to avoid troubling you in the least with truth too severely personal."[9] In grand contrast, he described his own preaching ministry with blistering militancy (warning: it takes some time to calm down after hearing what is a mere *description* of his preaching): "We do not go out snow-balling on Sundays, we go fire-balling; we ought to hurl grenades into the enemy's ranks."[10] You may want to take a moment to recompose yourself now.

As well as distinguishing preaching from mere data-dumping, Spurgeon was clear that "to preach" is not the same thing as "to moralise." "Remember," he told his students, "you are not sent to whiten tombs, but to open them."[11] The transformation he longed for in his listeners was not merely at the superficial behavioral level (though he wanted to see godly behavior), but also at the very core of their being. Through preaching the gospel, he wanted to see the spiritually dead come to new life in Christ, and the living to become more gloriously Christlike and alive. And through such gospel preaching, he was clear, the evils of the times will be addressed: the vicious will become peace-loving and upright, the proud humble, the greedy generous, and the addicts freed.

> We have only to preach the living gospel, and the whole of it, to meet the whole of the evils of the times. The gospel, if it were fully received through the whole earth, would purge away all slavery, end all war, and put down all drunkenness and all social evils; in fact you cannot conceive a moral curse which it would not remove, and even physical evils, since many of them arise incidentally from sin, would be greatly mitigated and some of them for ever abolished.[12]

Only the gospel of Christ has power to effect that sort of radical transformation in human hearts and lives. But I should explain myself here. As far as I can tell, in all his forty packed years of preaching, he never missed an opportunity to address the unbelievers in his hearing. He was consistently and strongly evangelistic in his preaching. However, in the main it is

---

[9] *ARM*, 118. Cf. C. H. Spurgeon, *The Soul Winner: How to Lead Sinners to the Saviour* (New York: Fleming H. Revell, 1895), 55.
[10] Spurgeon, *The Soul Winner*, 69.
[11] *Lectures*, 2:230.
[12] *S&T: 1877*, 71.

not possible to divide his evangelistic from his pastoral preaching: the one gospel was his message for all, believer and unbeliever alike.

Spurgeon's Exegesis

Evangelicals today who have read a few Spurgeon sermons commonly have mixed reactions. On the one hand, they typically express deep admiration for the passion, the richness, and the sheer artistry that still shines through, just in the written copies. On the other, they often express a reluctant discomfort that he was not more rigorously expository in his approach. Some clarification is necessary to understand and appreciate how and why Spurgeon preached as he did.

In his sermons, Spurgeon would almost invariably take a very short text or single verse of Scripture on which to preach. However, it would be entirely misleading to read such a Spurgeon sermon and imagine it was the only biblical content he gave his congregation. In fact, he was quite critical of those who "deliver much of the teaching of Holy Scripture by picking out verse by verse, and holding these up at random. The process resembles that of showing a house by exhibiting separate bricks."[13] So, in addition to his sermon, in another part of the church service Spurgeon used to give a separate verse-by-verse exposition on the portion of Scripture from which his preaching text would be taken. This, he believed, gave him "an opportunity of saying many things which are not of sufficient importance to become the theme of a whole sermon."[14] It also enabled him to give his people, in addition to the pastoral sword-thrust of his sermon, a more bird's-eye view of Scripture. Through the exposition they could appreciate the glorious coherence and the broader interconnections between different verses, chapters, and themes of Scripture.[15] Spurgeon spent much time studying in the preparation of these expositions: more time, in fact, than he would give to the preparation of the sermon itself.[16] He wanted, after all, to give a full exposition of the passage, and to be "sure in our public expositions that *obscure and involved sentences are explained*. To overleap difficulties, and only expound what is already clear, is to make commenting ridiculous."[17] And yet even more than that was involved, for he held that even here the

---

13 *Lectures*, 4:43.
14 *Lectures*, 4:45.
15 *Lectures*, 4:46.
16 *Lectures*, 4:46.
17 *Lectures*, 4:52.

people should not simply be given a biblical theology lecture: the exposition, as well as the sermon, had to be applied throughout to the hearts of the congregation.[18]

Spurgeon's congregation would, therefore, hear verse-by-verse exposition of Scripture every week. However, Spurgeon tended to dislike planned sermon series in which a preacher seeks to expound whole books of Scripture, passage by passage. He was quite aware that in this he was setting himself against many of the greatest preachers who have done just that; yet he felt that very few preachers possess the talent to carry off such series. Most would simply bore their people.

> It is even said of that wonderful expositor, Joseph Caryl, that he commenced his famous lectures upon Job with eight hundred hearers, and closed the book with only eight! . . . Ordinarily, and for ordinary men, it seems to me that pre-arranged discourses are a mistake, are never more than an apparent benefit, and generally a real mischief. Surely to go through a long epistle must require a great deal of genius in the preacher, and demand a world of patience on the part of the hearers. I am moved by a yet deeper consideration in what I have now said: it strikes me that many a truly living, earnest preacher, would feel a programme to be a fetter. Should the preacher announce for next Lord's day a topic full of joy, requiring liveliness and exaltation of spirit, it is very possible that he may, from various causes, find himself in a sad and burdened state of mind; nevertheless, he must put the new wine into his old bottle, and go up to the wedding feast wearing his sackcloth and ashes, and worst of all, this he may be bound to repeat for a whole month. Is this quite as it should be? It is important that the speaker should be in tune with his theme, but how is this to be secured unless the election of the topic is left to influences which shall work at the time? A man is not a steam engine, to run on metals, and it is unwise to fix him in one groove. Very much of the preacher's power will lie in his whole soul being in accord with the subject.[19]

All this was part of his basic idea that preaching must transform lives and not merely educate minds. Long sermon series are certainly educational, but they are not designed to address the *immediate* situation of the congregation. Indeed, they cannot. And this concerned Spurgeon, who counseled his students that "although all Scripture is good and profitable,

---

[18] *Lectures*, 4:54.
[19] *Lectures*, 1:100.

yet it is not all equally appropriate for every occasion."[20] He therefore gave great care each week to choosing a text that seemed most fitting for his people *on that precise occasion*. "I frequently sit hour after hour praying and waiting for a subject," he once explained, adding, "this is the main part of my study."[21] He wanted to consider the condition of his hearers, their spiritual state, and then "prescribe the medicine adapted to the current disease, or prepare the food suitable for the prevailing necessity."[22] It even meant that (very rarely) he was prepared to change his text on the day itself. This happened once at New Park Street when, giving out the hymn before the sermon, he opened his Bible to find his text "when on the opposite page another passage of Scripture sprang upon me like a lion from a thicket, with vastly more power than I had felt when considering the text which I had chosen."[23]

What, then, are we to make of Spurgeon's lack of rigorous expository style in his sermons? First, it needs to be seen within its context: in an age when there was very little straight expository preaching, Spurgeon gave his congregation a textual commentary that would frame his sermons. Second, his practice of preaching (which could never be perfect) reveals a theology of preaching that needs to be heeded. As Helmut Thielicke put it:

> It would be well for a time like ours to learn from this man. For our preaching is, to be sure, largely correct, exegetically "legitimate," workmanlike and tidy; but it is also remarkably dead and lacking in infectious power. . . .
>
> . . . The dogmatician, the exegete, and also the professor of practical theology (the preceptor of the homiletical nursery) may often be impelled to wield their blue pencils; the aesthete may often see red and the liturgiologist turn purple when they read his sermons and hear what he did. . . .
>
> Such critics ought to see in this man Spurgeon the shepherd who was content to allow his robe—including his clerical robe—to be torn to tatters by thorns and sharp stones as he clambered after the lost sheep, at times seeming to be engaged more in training for a cross-country race than in liturgical exercises. Worldly preaching is impossible without having the earth leave its traces on a man's wardrobe.[24]

---

20 *Lectures*, 1:84–85.
21 *Lectures*, 1:88.
22 *Lectures*, 1:90.
23 *Lectures*, 1:95.
24 Helmut Thielicke, *Encounter with Spurgeon* (London: James Clarke, 1964), 2, 40–41.

Advice for Preachers

With that in mind, what advice would Spurgeon give the preacher who aims, as he did, to woo for Christ? The rest of this chapter is dedicated to answering that question.

Preach Christ

First, the preacher must *clearly* and *faithfully* preach Christ. He is "Scripture's great theme" and the bridegroom that the servants are sent forth to make known.[25] By "Christ," Spurgeon meant "not merely his example and the ethical precepts of his teaching, but his atoning blood, his wondrous satisfaction made for human sin, and the grand doctrine of 'believe and live.'"[26] In other words, "to preach Christ" involves preaching *all* the doctrines that set him forth. It is a stretching and not a limiting mandate for the preacher. Christ must, after all, be preached for who he is and what he has done in his entirety.[27] But Spurgeon preferred to speak of preaching "Christ" than preaching "the gospel," "the truth," or anything else, because of how easily we reduce "the gospel" or "the truth" to an impersonal system. Christ himself is, in person, the way, the truth, and the life; the glory of God; the life and delight of the saints; the Bridegroom that the bride is invited to enjoy.

Throughout his ministry, Spurgeon hammered away unrelentingly as, with passion and color, he urged every preacher to preach Christ. To get some sense of this, it is worth taking a moment to enjoy a few examples:

> I would never preach a sermon—the Lord forgive me if I do—which is not full to overflowing with my Master. I know one who said I was always on the old string, and he would come and hear me no more; but if I preached a sermon without Christ in it, he would come. Ah! he will never come while this tongue moves, for a sermon without Christ in it—a Christless sermon! A brook without water; a cloud without rain; a well which mocks the traveller; a tree twice dead, plucked up by the root; a sky without a sun; a night without a star. It were a realm of death—a place of mourning for angels and laughter for devils.[28]

> Talking this day with a brother in the ministry, one who has been many years a preacher, he was telling me that he had been to the British Museum

25 *MTP*, 57:496.
26 *MTP*, 27:598.
27 *S&T: 1881*, 35.
28 *MTP*, 10:139.

library, looking after sermons upon Christ, and in turning the books over, he said, he thought he had found pretty well five hundred upon any other subject to one upon the Lord Jesus! Perhaps he was wrong in his estimate; but even supposing he had found but five upon other subjects to one upon the Lord Jesus, would not that account for the fact of the lamentations that are made about the leanness of the pulpit? Leave Christ out? O my brethren, better leave the pulpit out altogether. If a man can preach one sermon without mentioning Christ's name in it, it ought to be his last, certainly the last that any Christian ought to go to hear him preach.[29]

That sermon which does not lead to Christ, or of which Jesus Christ is not the top and the bottom, is a sort of sermon that will make the devils in hell to laugh, but might make the angels of God to weep.[30]

No other subject ever does produce such effects as this. The Spirit of God bears no witness to Christless sermons. Leave Jesus out of your preaching, and the Holy Spirit will never come upon you. Why should he? Has he not come on purpose that he may testify of Christ? Did not Jesus say, "He shall glorify me: for he shall receive of mine, and shall shew it unto you"? Yes, the subject was Christ, and nothing but Christ, and such is the teaching which the Spirit of God will own.[31]

You do not really preach the gospel if you leave Christ out; if he be omitted, it is not the gospel. You may invite men to listen to your message, but you are only inviting them to gaze upon an empty table unless Christ is the very centre and substance of all that you set before them.[32]

The motto of all true servants of God must be, "We preach Christ, and him crucified." A sermon without Christ in it is like a loaf of bread without any flour in it. No Christ in your sermon, sir? Then go home, and never preach again until you have something worth preaching.[33]

Yes, it is Christ, Christ, Christ whom we have to preach; and if we leave him out, we leave out the very soul of the gospel. Christless sermons make merriment for hell. Christless preachers, Christless Sunday-school teachers, Christless class-leaders, Christless tract-distributors—what are

---

29 *MTP*, 13:489.
30 *MTP*, 25:634.
31 *MTP*, 26:315.
32 *MTP*, 48:325.
33 *MTP*, 50:431.

all these doing? They are simply setting the mill to grind without putting any grist into the hopper, so all their labour is in vain. If you leave Jesus Christ out, you are simply beating the air, or going to war without any weapon with which you can smite the foe.[34]

Of all I would wish to say this is the sum; my brethren, preach CHRIST, always and evermore. He is the whole gospel. His person, offices, and work must be our one great, all-comprehending theme. The world needs still to be told of its Saviour, and of the way to reach him.[35]

The best way to preach sinners to Christ is to preach Christ to sinners.[36]

Spurgeon was simply urging upon others what he himself practiced. In his very first sermon in the Metropolitan Tabernacle, on March 25, 1861, he announced, "I would propose that the subject of the ministry of this house, as long as this platform shall stand, and as long as this house shall be frequented by worshippers, shall be the person of Jesus Christ."[37] And in his thirty years of pastoring there, he did not stray from that theme. These are his last words from the pulpit, dated June 7, 1891:

It is heaven to serve Jesus. I am a recruiting sergeant, and I would fain find a few recruits at this moment. Every man must serve somebody: we have no choice as to that fact. Those who have no master are slaves to themselves. Depend upon it, you will either serve Satan or Christ, either self or the Saviour. You will find sin, self, Satan, and the world to be hard masters; but if you wear the livery of Christ, you will find him so meek and lowly of heart that you will find rest unto your souls. He is the most magnanimous of captains. There never was his like among the choicest of princes. He is always to be found in the thickest part of the battle. When the wind blows cold he always takes the bleak side of the hill. The heaviest end of the cross lies ever on his shoulders. If he bids us carry a burden, he carries it also. If there is anything that is gracious, generous, kind, and tender, yea lavish and superabundant in love, you always find it in him. These forty years and more have I served him, blessed be his name! and I have had nothing but love from him. I would be glad to continue yet another forty years in the same dear service here below if so it pleased him.

---

[34] *MTP*, 58:63.
[35] *Lectures*, 1:82.
[36] *Lectures*, 2:272.
[37] *MTP*, 7:169.

His service is life, peace, joy. Oh, that you would enter on it at once! God help you to enlist under the banner of Jesus even this day! Amen.[38]

Spurgeon was emphatic that keeping Christ central, prominent, and clear was the reason for the fruitfulness of his ministry. "If I had preached any other than the doctrine of Christ crucified, I should years ago have scattered my audience to the winds of heaven. But the old theme is always new, always fresh, always attractive. Preach Jesus Christ."[39]

To explain his approach to preaching Christ from Scripture, Spurgeon often told the story of a conversation between an immature young preacher and a venerable divine. When the novice asked the old minister what he thought of the sermon he had just preached, the minister told him it had been a "very poor sermon indeed" because "there was no Christ in it."

> "Well," said the young man, "Christ was not in the text; we are not to be preaching Christ always, we must preach what is in the text." So the old man said, "Don't you know young man that from every town, and every village, and every little hamlet in England, wherever it may be, there is a road to London?" "Yes," said the young man. "Ah!" said the old divine "and so from every text in Scripture, there is a road to the metropolis of the Scriptures, that is Christ. And my dear brother, your business is when you get to a text, to say, 'Now what is the road to Christ?' and then preach a sermon, running along the road towards the great metropolis—Christ. And," said he "I have never yet found a text that had not got a road to Christ in it, and if I ever do find one that has not a road to Christ in it, I will make one; I will go over hedge and ditch but I would get at my Master, for the sermon cannot do any good unless there is a savour of Christ in it."[40]

This statement and approach have, understandably, attracted a certain amount of critique from biblical scholars. Spurgeon's willingness to "go over hedge and ditch" makes it sound like he is willing to play fast and loose with the text just so he can get to his desired theological destination. Sidney Greidanus, for example, concluded that Spurgeon's

> single-minded concern to preach Jesus Christ often leads him to reading Christ back into the Old Testament text. He generally uses the life of Jesus

---

[38] MTP, 37:323–24.
[39] MTP, 29:233–34.
[40] NPSP, 5:140.

as a grid for interpreting the Old Testament. In other words, he frequently fails to do justice to the literal sense and the historical context of the Old Testament passages. He does not ask about the intention of the original author; he does not enquire about the message for Israel. Instead, he tends to use the Old Testament as a "springboard" for his message about Jesus Christ.[41]

Though I would not claim that Spurgeon always got his exegesis straight, this criticism is rather unfair. He did indeed have a "single-minded concern to preach Jesus Christ," but his sermons *commonly* address the historical context and the original intention of the human author.[42] Perhaps a good part of the real problem here is that Spurgeon simply understood the relationship between Christ and the historical/literal meaning of texts *differently*. Rather than ever needing to read Christ "back in," he felt he was simply trying to understand how the text was *originally* intended to proclaim Christ. Take, for instance, his comments on Psalm 45, concerning the marriage of "the king":

> Some here see Solomon and Pharaoh's daughter only—they are short-sighted; others see both Solomon and Christ—they are cross-eyed; well-focussed spiritual eyes see here Jesus only, or if Solomon be present at all, it must be like those hazy shadows of passers-by which cross the face of the camera, and therefore are dimly traceable upon a photographic landscape. "The King," the God whose throne is for ever and ever, is no mere mortal and his everlasting dominion is not bounded by Lebanon and Egypt's river.[43]

Greidanus also claims that Spurgeon's "single-minded desire to preach Jesus Christ isolates the person and work of Christ from the person and work of God the Father."[44] Certainly we all are inconsistent, yet this fails to account for how clear Spurgeon was that faithful preaching of Jesus Christ the Son of God *is being Trinitarian*. As Spurgeon himself put it, "We will preach Christ as the sinner's Saviour, the Spirit of God as applying Christ's truth to the soul, and God the Father in His infinite sovereignty saving whom He wills."[45] The

---

41 Sidney Greidanus, *Preaching Christ from the Old Testament: A Contemporary Hermeneutical Method* (Grand Rapids: Eerdmans, 1999), 160.
42 See, for example, *MTP*, 12:481–82; 18:157–58; 21:145–46; 25:467; 29:145; 35:277–78; 41:457–58.
43 C. H. Spurgeon, *The Treasury of David: Psalms 27–57*, vol. 2 (London: Marshall Brothers, n.d.), 315.
44 Greidanus, *Preaching Christ from the Old Testament*, 162.
45 *Autobiog.*, 3:3–4.

will of the Father and the ministry of the Spirit are to witness to Jesus Christ, known by the Spirit as the way to the Father. And it is not as if Spurgeon kept the Father and the Spirit only implicit in his ministry. To preach Christ faithfully, Spurgeon was repeatedly lengthy and explicit in his teaching on both the Father and the Spirit.

> We ought to declare that grand doctrine of the Father's love towards His people from before all worlds. His sovereign choice of them, His covenant purposes concerning them, and His immutable promises to them, must all be uttered with trumpet tongue. Coupled with this, the true evangelist must never fail to set forth the beauties of the person of Christ, the glory of His offices, the completeness of His work, and, above all, the efficacy of His blood. Whatever we omit, this must be in the most forcible manner proclaimed again and again. That is no gospel which has not Christ in it; and the modern idea of preaching THE TRUTH instead of Christ, is a wicked device of Satan. Nor is this all, for as there are three Persons in the Godhead, we must be careful that They all have due honour in our ministry. The Holy Spirit's work in regeneration, in sanctification, and in preservation, must be always magnified from our pulpit. Without His power, our ministry is a dead letter, and we cannot expect His arm to be made bare unless we honour Him day by day.[46]

Preach Clearly and Beautifully

Next, if he is to be preached faithfully, the Christ who is the light and glory of God must be preached both *clearly* and *beautifully*.

Spurgeon intensely disliked the flowery, overblown oratory and affectation he associated especially with the "gentlemanly" (or, as he saw it, "effete") Oxford movement.[47] It stank, for him, of self-involvement, something entirely at odds with the faithful minister's duty to serve and feed the people. "Some would impress us by their depth of thought, when it is merely a love of big words. To hide plain things in dark sentences, is sport rather than service for God."[48] Nor can pretentious, prettified talk penetrate hearts and so transform lives. Proud words cannot produce humble people. Spurgeon thus spoke, quite deliberately, in everyday, down-to-earth, "plain Saxon."[49]

---

[46] *Autobiog.*, 2:228.
[47] The Oxford Movement, which started in the 1830s, was a Catholic revival movement in the Church of England.
[48] *ARM*, 353.
[49] *MTP*, 59:319–20.

> Better far give the people masses of unprepared truth in the rough, like pieces of meat from a butcher's block, chopped off anyhow, bone and all, and even dropped down in the sawdust, than ostentatiously and delicately hand them out upon a china dish a delicious slice of nothing at all, decorated with the parsley of poetry, and flavoured with the sauce of affectation.[50]

More than simplicity of language, such clear preaching requires from the preacher lucidity of thought. He must convey the great truths of God, without simplifying and distorting them, with clarity and comprehensibility. And in this Spurgeon was, perhaps, unrivaled. Hear the enviable oomph with which he puts it: "Christ said, 'Feed My sheep . . . Feed My lambs.' Some preachers, however, put the food so high that neither lambs nor sheep can reach it. They seem to have read the text, 'Feed My giraffes.'"[51]

He was also highly aware of both the power and the allure of beauty—an awareness that told in his enjoyment of beauty throughout life. Spurgeon therefore hated the thought of preaching or teaching truth in a dull, plodding manner. The truth is, in fact, beautiful. Christ, after all, *is* beauty itself. The truth must then be *shown* to be beautiful if it is to be proclaimed faithfully. Commenting on Psalm 45, he wrote, "King Jesus deserves to be praised not with random, ranting ravings, but with the sweetest and most skilful music of the best trained choristers." This sort of praise that glorifies God can only come from sanctified hearts, since the "purest hearts in the spiritual temple are the most harmonious songsters in the ears of God."[52] Yet it is not *just* a matter of having hearts in tune: the *words* they use matter too.

> Jesus is so emphatically lovely that words must be doubled, strained, yea, exhausted before he can be described. . . . Love delights to see the Beloved arrayed as beseemeth his excellency; she weeps as she sees him in the garments of humiliation, she rejoices to behold him in the vestments of his exaltation. Our precious Christ can never be made too much of.[53]

It would be a mistake, then, simply to think of Spurgeon as a plain, clear preacher. That could suggest *bare*, *stark*, or *thin*—words that really

---

[50] *Lectures*, 1:77.
[51] William Williams, *Personal Reminiscences of Charles Haddon Spurgeon* (London: Passmore & Alabaster, 1895), 145.
[52] Spurgeon, *The Treasury of David: Psalms 27–57*, 2:315.
[53] Spurgeon, *The Treasury of David: Psalms 27–57*, 2:316–17.

won't do at all when thinking of Spurgeon. Pretentious he was not, but colorful he most certainly was, his sermons and writings glowing with eye-catching, picture-filled richness.

Stand in Christ's Stead

Preachers who woo for Christ, aiming at divorcing hearts from sin and wedding them to Christ, must view themselves as *standing in Christ's stead*. As he once stood in our place, so we now get to stand in his, sent forth into the world with his gospel just as he was sent by his Father (John 20:21). Preachers are heralds and ambassadors for Christ, pleading for him even as he now pleads for us, urging people to be reconciled to God (2 Cor. 5:20). In arguing this, Spurgeon was making a fine-tuned but profoundly significant point: preachers "are not only labouring *for* Christ, but *in His stead*."[54]

Practically, this means that preachers must *love* the sinners they address, as Christ does. They cannot show partiality, "speaking up" to the educated, fawning on the wealthy, or pandering to any, just giving what they want to hear. Pleading in Christ's stead means they must not bully, but, like Christ, they must "tenderly persuade." And they must do so with Christ's own holy sympathy, feeling his desire to bless them, as well as his sorrow that they might not enter into his joy. They must share his patience with them "because of His Divine long-suffering." They must, in other words, share Christ's own passion and compassion—and that means sharing Christ's own pain as they *"fill up that which is behind of the sufferings of Christ for His body's sake, which is the Church."*[55]

> I think, again, that *we shall do well to stand towards Christ as those who are conscious of His power and presence*. Brethren, our Lord is with us. . . . When we get into the pulpit, let us look Christward and lean Christward. What a wondrous place the pulpit is when Jesus is there! In the study, when we sit down, and begin to rub our foreheads, and anxiously enquire, "What shall we preach about?" let us turn towards our Lord, and pray with our window open towards His cross and His throne. May we ever feel an influence drawing us Christward when the Bible is open before us! If it be so, our weakness will all vanish, for His strength will be remembered.[56]

---

[54] *ARM*, 380, my emphasis.
[55] *ARM*, 381–83.
[56] *ARM*, 387.

It also means that, as it is for Christ himself, the glory of God must be the preacher's chief desire and object. Spurgeon was repeatedly emphatic with the students of his Pastors' College about this.[57] "Once more, if we are to be robed in the power of the Lord, *we must feel an intense longing for the glory of God, and the salvation of the sons of men.*"[58] God is glorified in the salvation of sinners and the building up of the saints, and so preachers must seek those things. However, those things are not the preacher's *primary* business: God will be glorified if his truth is faithfully preached *even if none are saved or built up.* "THE grand object of the Christian ministry is the glory of God. Whether souls are converted or not, if Jesus Christ be faithfully preached, the minister has not labored in vain, for he is a sweet savour unto God as well in them that perish as in them that are saved."[59]

Seek to Embody the Text

In order to serve as a faithful ambassador of Christ, and to dare to stand in his stead, the preacher must *embody* the new life Christ offers. He should both know *and enjoy* the truth he seeks to share if he is to share it successfully. "The word should come from the minister like bread hot from the oven, or better still, like a seed with life in it; not as a parched grain with the germ dead and killed."[60] If a preacher does not believe the gospel he proclaims, God *may* still use him in spite of himself, but that preacher's Christlessness only nullifies his own message. "The best of food may be rendered unpalatable through the slovenliness of the cook."[61] But if we preachers enjoy close communion with Christ, living in Spirit-filled dependence on the Father, then we will be conformed into his likeness and find our very presence a sermon. Then we shall know and utter the mind of God and embody the gospel we proclaim. "Do you not love to hear a brother speak who abides in fellowship with Jesus?" Spurgeon asked. "Even a few minutes with such a man is refreshing, for, like his Master, his paths drop fatness. Dwell in the truth and let the truth dwell in you. Be baptized into its spirit and influence that you may impart thereof to others."[62]

But Spurgeon wanted to press the point home further. Not only must the preacher generally embody new life in Christ; he must, more

---

[57] *Autobiog.*, 2:148.
[58] *ARM*, 352.
[59] *Lectures*, 2:264. Cf. *ARM*, 299.
[60] *MTP*, 25:429.
[61] *S&T: 1883*, 92.
[62] *S&T: 1877*, 80. Cf. *ARM*, 350.

specifically, embody *the actual text he expounds*. Spurgeon himself always preached best, he found, if he managed to "bathe" or "soak" in his text, to let the text soak into him. "It softens me, or hardens me, or does whatever it ought to do to me, and then I can talk about it."[63] He wanted not just to comprehend but to *feel* and *share* his text's indignation at sin, its hope in God, its comfort in Christ, or whatever its subject might be. Only then, Spurgeon found, could he find both the right words and tone to accurately convey both the message and the spirit of the text.

Spurgeon took this so seriously that he would not preach upon, say, the joy of the Lord when feeling downcast, or the saint's frustration at indwelling sin when rejoicing in his own cleansing by Christ.[64] The danger he feared was that in that instance he would be unconvincing (and a "lukewarm sermon sickens every healthy mind").[65] Or, worse, he must become insincere and affected. And that thought revolted him. He knew that when a preacher *feels* the truth of what he proclaims, it works powerfully on the hearts of others. But feigned feeling in the preacher is both deceitful and deeply dangerous, and tends either to glorify the preacher or, when detected, revolt the people from the very message he holds out.[66]

Preach Christ in a Christly Manner

All this advice was summed up in an address he gave at the Pastors' College in 1881, titled "Preach Christ in a Christly Manner." His students were all expecting him to urge them to preach Christ, and he did not disappoint: "Ministers of the gospel, let Christ be your *subject*, and let Christ be your *model*: find in him not only the truth you utter, but the way and life of your utterance."[67] And yet, he added, "As for Christ's being our subject, I have spoken upon that theme so many times that there is the less need on this occasion to dwell upon it at any length."[68] His focus in this address would be on Christ as the *model* for the preacher.

Christ was zealous for his Father's business. Zeal for God's house consumed him so thoroughly that he was in great distress until his mission (that is, his excruciating death) could be accomplished (Luke 12:50; John 2:17). As such, argued Spurgeon, Christ always preached *solemnly*. "There

---

63 *ARM*, 124–25.
64 *ARM*, 65.
65 *S&T: 1881*, 101.
66 *Lectures*, 1:49–50.
67 *S&T: 1881*, 35.
68 *S&T: 1881*, 35.

was weight about every word that he said, meaning in every gesture, force in every tone. He was never a trifler."[69] Christ, in other words, took in all seriousness the eternal gravity of his task in all his dealing with people. Yet Spurgeon knew how easily that "seriousness" could be misinterpreted by men who are not full of the joy of the Lord. And so he added:

> Although our Lord always spoke solemnly, yet never drearily, there is a pleasant interest about his words, for he preached glad tidings *joyfully*. It was evidently his meat and his drink to do the will of him that sent him. He delighted in his ministry, and in it he found refreshment. I cannot imagine our Saviour during those three years wearing the aspect of one who was tired of his work, or as speaking merely because he was expected to do so, in a dull, monotonous, lifeless manner. His heart was in his sermons, and parables, and gracious talks; he loved to be God's ambassador, and would not have exchanged his office to rule empires.[70]

Christ also preached *meekly*. He was not pompous or overbearing, but spoke to sinners as a kind friend to friends. Thus, "scolding in the pulpit, bitterness in conversation, asperity of manner, and domineering over others are not for us, for they are not Christly things."[71] Of course, that too could be misinterpreted, and so Spurgeon added that while Christ preached meekly, he also did so *courageously*. His gentle and loving "meekness" cannot be confused with tame harmlessness. He would rebuke sin roundly and not shy from speaking of hellfire. But Spurgeon's point was that in all Christ's fearless proclamation of the truth, *bold* never meant "brutal," and *courageous* never meant "callous."

Christ was also uncommonly *simple* in his use of language. For all his peerless and divine wisdom, he used words that can be readily understood by all. That being the case, well-educated preachers who would preach like him must be very careful to wear their learning lightly. Not that they should lay aside any of their actual wisdom: it is simply that they should use it all to serve the people and not their own egos or reputations. "Aspire to be understood rather than to be admired. Seek not to produce a wondering but an instructed audience."[72] Once again, Spurgeon had a counterbalance to this piece of advice: "simple" should not mean "vacuous" or "shallow." The call

---

[69] *S&T: 1881*, 36.
[70] *S&T: 1881*, 36–37.
[71] *S&T: 1881*, 37.
[72] *S&T: 1881*, 38–39.

for simplicity is not an excuse for the intellectually lazy: "Let your teaching be clear as crystal, but deep as the sea."[73] In plain language, preachers must hold out profound truths. Never vapid or trivial, to be like Christ they must be as solid in matter as they are simple in manner.

Finally—and this, Spurgeon believed, was the most distinguishing mark of the Savior's preaching—Christ did all this with an intense *love* for both God and his hearers. His theology was built on prayer and led to worship; his "preaching was his heart set to words."[74] Spurgeon thus urged his students to preach devotedly and prayerfully. "This is the way to preach. Pray the divine message into yourself, and then preach it out of yourself. Speak with God for men, and then speak with men for God."[75] Preachers must also share Christ's heartfelt affection for sinners so that they truly love the ones to whom they proclaim God's grace and glory. This will transform how they speak to them, as it did for Christ. "When he has to speak sternly, as well as at every other time, his tenderness is apparent. He laments even while he condemns. If Jerusalem must be doomed, its sentence is pronounced by a voice that is choked for utterance."[76]

Christ, then, was the truest model as well as the truest subject of Christian preaching: "I hold up to you Jesus Christ as the model preacher. I hold up no man beside, and I earnestly advise you never to become slavish copyists of any living preachers. Do you reply that you need a living teacher? I reply that Jesus is a living model; for, blessed be God, he ever liveth."[77]

Spurgeon was addressing young preachers, but his counsel is fitting for all Christians. As we share the gospel with friends and neighbors, Spurgeon reminds us that it is Christ—in all the multifaceted glories of his person and work—who must be the focal point of our message and the treasure we offer. And as we do that, we will properly adorn our message as we share Christ's own zeal, Christ's own courageous meekness and simplicity, and Christ's own love for both God and neighbor.

---

[73] S&T: *1881*, 39.
[74] S&T: *1881*, 40.
[75] S&T: *1881*, 40.
[76] S&T: *1881*, 41.
[77] S&T: *1881*, 41.

PART 3

THE NEW BIRTH

CHAPTER 5

NEW BIRTH AND BAPTISM

Conversion

Spurgeon was raised in a Christian home, baptized as an infant by his grandfather, and, through his childhood, quite used to earnest conversation about spiritual matters, prayer, and reading the Bible and Puritan books. Yet he was not at that point a believer. By the time he was ten years old, he had fallen under a strong sense of guilt for his sin. He devoured those Puritan books for answers and yet for five years felt himself to be like Bunyan's pilgrim, carrying a heavy and depressing burden. He was trapped in darkness and despair. "What I wanted to know was, 'How can I get my sins forgiven?' . . . I panted and longed to understand how I might be saved."[1]

Then, when he was fifteen, in January 1850, walking to an unnamed place of worship in Colchester, he was caught in a snowstorm.[2] He turned down Artillery Street and walked into a small Primitive Methodist chapel

---

[1] *Autobiog.*, 1:105.

[2] The exact date is uncertain. Spurgeon believed that he was converted on January 6; however, there are reasons to think he may well have been mistaken and that January 13 is the true date. First, meteorological evidence indicates that there was snow over January 12–13, but not the previous weekend. Second, the Primitive Methodist circuit plan shows that Robert Eaglen was preaching in Colchester on January 13. Spurgeon always declared that the identity of the preacher whose ministry was used for his conversion was unknown to him. Yet three members of Artillery Street Chapel (including the senior church officer) testified that Robert Eaglen was the man, and this testimony was supported by other local Primitive Methodist ministers. Eaglen was even taken to meet Spurgeon a few years later, but having recovered from the "pulmonary consumption" which afflicted him in 1850, he had put on weight and was unrecognizable to Spurgeon. See D. Sheen, *Pastor C. H. Spurgeon: His Conversion, Career, and Coronation* (London: J. B. Knapp, 1892), 14–51; and T. McCoy, "The Evangelistic Ministry of C. H. Spurgeon: Implications for a Contemporary Model of Pastoral Evangelism" (PhD diss., Southern Baptist Theological Seminary, 1989), appendix D, 323–50.

there. A "very thin-looking man" went up into the pulpit to preach, and Spurgeon quickly felt that this preacher was "really stupid." Apparently he could not even rightly pronounce the words of his text, which was Isaiah 45:22, "Look unto me, and be ye saved, all the ends of the earth" (KJV). He began with these words:

> "My dear friends, this is a very simple text indeed. It says, 'Look.' Now lookin' don't take a deal of pains. It ain't liftin' your foot or your finger; it is just, 'Look.' Well, a man needn't go to College to learn to look. You may be the biggest fool, and yet you can look. A man needn't be worth a thousand a year to be able to look. Anyone can look; even a child can look. But then the text says, 'Look unto *Me*.' Ay!" said he, in broad Essex, "many on [*sic*] ye are lookin' to yourselves, but it's no use lookin' there. You'll never find any comfort in yourselves. Some look to God the Father. No, look to Him by-and-by. Jesus Christ says, 'Look unto *Me*.' Some on [*sic*] ye say, 'We must wait for the Spirit's workin'.' You have no business with that just now. Look to *Christ*. The text says. 'Look unto *Me*.'"[3]

After about ten minutes, with only twelve to fifteen people present, the preacher fixed his eyes on Spurgeon and spoke to him directly: "Young man, you look very miserable." Then, lifting up his hands, he shouted, "Young man, look to Jesus Christ. Look! Look! Look! You have nothin' to do but to look and live." At that, Spurgeon later wrote:

> I saw at once the way of salvation. I know not what else he said,—I did not take much notice of it,—I was so possessed with that one thought. Like as when the brazen serpent was lifted up, the people only looked and were healed, so it was with me. I had been waiting to do fifty things, but when I heard that word, "Look!" what a charming word it seemed to me! Oh! I looked until I could almost have looked my eyes away. There and then the cloud was gone, the darkness had rolled away, and that moment I saw the sun; and I could have risen that instant, and sung with the most enthusiastic of them, of the precious blood of Christ, and the simple faith which looks alone to Him.[4]

Ever since then, Spurgeon saw a number of essential features in his own experience of conversion, and the necessity of new birth would be of outstanding importance in his thought. It made him an evangelist. It was not that evan-

---

[3] *Autobiog.*, 1:106.
[4] *Autobiog.*, 1:106.

gelism came easily to him: naturally bookish and reticent, he envied those, he said, "who can go up to individuals, and talk to them with freedom about their souls. I do not always find myself able to do so."[5] Yet one of the clearest ways in which God glorifies himself is in the forgiveness and salvation of sinners, and so seeing conversions became one of Spurgeon's greatest ambitions. "I would sooner pluck one single brand from the burning than explain all mysteries," he declared. "To win a soul from going down into the pit, is a more glorious achievement than to be crowned in the arena of theological controversy as *Dr. Sufficientissimus*."[6] It meant that he would be constantly and exceptionally evangelistic throughout a forty-year ministry that was impressively fruitful. Tom Nettles has drawn together some of the vital statistics here:

> In 1853 the New Park Street membership numbered 313. By the end of 1860 the membership had risen to 1,494. Though some came from other congregations, the bulk of these was converted and added to the church by baptism. For the next ten years the church added an average of 448 persons per year with a net increase of 267 each year. By 1870 the membership stood at 4,165. By 1882 the membership reached 5,472. The last ten years of his ministry continued to see hundreds of additions with an average of 269 baptisms each year.[7]

Baptism

Spurgeon had not been brought up a Baptist, and he had been converted among pedobaptist Primitive Methodists. And yet a very few weeks after his conversion, he wrote to his father: "From the Scriptures, is it not apparent that, immediately upon receiving the Lord Jesus, it is a part of duty openly to profess him? I firmly believe and consider that baptism is the command of Christ, and shall not feel quite comfortable if I do not receive it."[8] Unable to find a Baptist church any nearer where he was then living, in Newmarket, Spurgeon arranged to be baptized by immersion in the river Lark, eight miles away. He had never actually seen an adult baptism before, but on May 3, 1850, at Isleham Ferry, he publicly confessed himself by baptism to be "a follower of the Lamb."[9]

---

[5] *Autobiog.*, 2:131.
[6] *Autobiog.*, 1:233.
[7] Tom Nettles, *Living by Revealed Truth: The Life and Pastoral Theology of Charles Haddon Spurgeon* (Fearn, Scotland: Mentor, 2013), 282.
[8] Letter to J. Spurgeon, January 30, 1850, in "C. H. Spurgeon. Letters to his father and mother, 1850–84," Angus Library, Regent's Park College, Oxford (D/SPU), No. 3.
[9] *Autobiog.*, 1:152.

Spurgeon's immersion as a believer in the river turned out to be no passing whim of youth. He remained a stalwart and passionate Baptist for the rest of his life. What matters for us here, though, is that his Baptistic convictions were not a mere matter of his having to choose a denominational alignment: they were an integral part of his theology of the Christian life.

At one level, one could say very simply that Spurgeon was a Baptist because he believed that to be the scriptural position.

> The particular doctrine adhered to by Baptists is that they acknowledge no authority unless it comes from the Word of God. . . . If we could find infant baptism in the Word of God, we should adopt it. It would help us out of a great difficulty, for it would take away from us that reproach which is attached to us,—that we are odd, and do not as other people do. But we have looked well through the Bible, and cannot find it.[10]

At another level, Spurgeon was a Baptist because he believed that baptism is essentially about an outward expression of the believer's *faith*, not a conferral of God's *grace*. And that made it obviously inappropriate to baptize infants. He consistently and repeatedly taught that baptism does not confer any grace. Rather, "*baptism is the avowal of faith*."[11] It is the moment obedient Christians begin to do their duty to their Lord and publicly confess him. It is the Christian soldier's pledge of allegiance to his new commander and the putting on of his new regimental uniform: "It is best to begin the Christian life with thorough consecration. . . . This should be one of the earliest forms of our worship of our Master—this total resignation of ourselves to him. According to his word, the first announcement of our faith should be by baptism."[12] Spurgeon could also speak of baptism as "the outward sign and emblem" of the washing away of the believer's sin.[13] He could even describe it as "a bond betwixt me and my Master."[14] Yet those things were true only because of the believer's *faith*: the believer's sin is washed away because he has believed; he has a bond with Christ because he has believed. Baptism itself has not done these things: faith has.

To clarify, Spurgeon added that "baptism is also *Faith's taking her proper*

---

10 *Autobiog.*, 1:155.
11 *MTP*, 10:326.
12 *MTP*, 26:7.
13 *MTP*, 10:326.
14 Letter to his mother, May 1, 1850, in C. H. Spurgeon, *The Letters of Charles Haddon Spurgeon* (London: Marshall Brothers, 1923), 21–22.

place."[15] Left to ourselves, and knowing that baptism does not confer any grace, we could wonder what the point of it is, and if we should bother. But baptism is a chance for faith to step up and do what Christ has so obviously commanded, whether or not we understand the reason why. Loyal soldiers do not ask why; they act. "The very simplicity and apparent uselessness of the ordinance should make the believer say, 'Therefore I do it because it becomes the better test to me of my obedience to my Master.'"[16]

Because he saw baptism as faith stepping forward and acting, Spurgeon particularly enjoyed using martial imagery in association with baptism. One image especially seemed to capture his meaning: Julius Caesar's crossing of the Rubicon River, which marked the border of Italy. That crossing symbolized the commencement of his war with Pompey and the Senate. There could be no going back after that. Just so, Spurgeon felt, baptism is the crossing of a Rubicon, symbolizing open war against the world, the flesh, and the Devil. "If Cæsar crosses the Rubicon, there will never be peace between him and the Senate again. He draws his sword, and he throws away his scabbard. Such is the act of baptism to the believer. It is the burning of the boats."[17]

Spurgeon's Objections to Pedobaptism

Knowing Spurgeon's beliefs, visitors to his house in Clapham, London, must surely have been surprised to see in his garden a baptismal font clearly designed for the baptism of infants. Had they asked about it (as he hoped they would), he would have turned to them with a grin, explaining that it was "one of the spoils of the Holy War," removed from a High Church building taken over by Baptists. Having become a birdbath, "it was at least unable ever again to assist in deluding people into the errors of baptismal regeneration."[18]

Spurgeon maintained a high regard for many who believed in infant baptism, not least Calvin, the vast majority of the Puritans, Wesley, Whitefield—and, in his own day, Bishop J. C. Ryle. Yet he fiercely opposed it as an open door to "popery."[19] The rise of Anglo-Catholicism in the nineteenth century had led to a mushrooming of belief in baptismal regeneration, and Spurgeon saw infant baptism inevitably luring people into that.

---

15 *MTP*, 10:326.
16 *MTP*, 10:327. Cf. *Autobiog.*, 1:154.
17 *Autobiog.*, 1:149–50. Cf. *MTP*, 19:353.
18 *Autobiog.*, 2:295.
19 *Autobiog.*, 2:217.

> I am persuaded that so long as infant baptism is practised in any Christian church, Popery will have a door set wide open for its return. . . . As long as you give baptism to an unregenerate child, people will imagine that it must do the child good; for they will ask, If it does not do it any good, why is it baptised? The statement that it puts children into the covenant, or renders them members of the visible church, is only a veiled form of the fundamental error of Baptismal Regeneration.[20]

On June 5, 1864, he fired one of his most significant volleys against infant baptism in a sermon titled "Baptismal Regeneration." Referring to it as "the great error which we have to contend with throughout England," he challenged evangelicals in the Church of England for their acquiescence in what he believed was a dangerous and erroneous practice.[21] "It is a most fearful fact," he declared, "that *in no age since the Reformation has Popery made such fearful strides in England as during the last few years.*"[22] So seriously did he take the issue that in the sermon he began to wax apocalyptic: "It may be that on this ground Armageddon shall be fought. Here shall come the great battle between Christ and his saints on the one hand, and the world, and forms, and ceremonies, on the other."[23]

All this will no doubt make many a Baptist stand and cheer, and many a pedobaptist groan with misunderstood frustration. Yet, for both, Spurgeon's evangelical *rationale* is deeply revealing. In "Baptismal Regeneration" Spurgeon gave two essential reasons for opposing infant baptism:

First, to give even the *impression* that dropping water on a head can save a soul undermines entirely the gospel's call for people to be born again. "We meet with persons who, when we tell them that they must be born again, assure us that they were born again when they were baptized."[24] In other words, infant baptism blinds people to their need for a new birth, replacing it with a ritualism that only confirms people in their natural, faithless religiosity. It creates a religion, said Spurgeon, that "seems to me to be the most mechanical religion now existing, and to be on a par with the praying windmills of Thibet, or the climbing up and down of Pilate's staircase to which Luther subjected himself in the days of his darkness."[25]

Second, infant baptism not only conceals our need to be born again; it

---

20 *MTP*, 19:556.
21 *MTP*, 10:315.
22 *MTP*, 10:322.
23 *MTP*, 10:328.
24 *MTP*, 10:321.
25 *MTP*, 10:318.

also draws people to trust in something other than Christ. Countless unbelievers, baptized as infants, could think themselves saved because of their baptism, and not because of Christ. And so, Spurgeon urged, "Away from all the tag-rags, wax candles, and millinery of Puseyism! away from all the gorgeous pomp of Popery! away from the fonts of Church-of-Englandism! we bid you turn your eyes to that naked cross, where hangs as a bleeding man the Son of God."[26] Indeed, a few weeks later Spurgeon followed up "Baptismal Regeneration" with a sermon devoted wholly to this theme. Titled "Children Brought to Christ, Not to the Font," it spoke of the infant baptismal font essentially as a rival to Christ, and of people putting their faith in one or the other:[27]

> I stand here this day to cry, "Come ye to the cross, not to the font." . . . The font is a mockery and an imposition if it be put before Christ. If you have baptism after you have come to Christ, well and good, but to point you to it either as being Christ, or as being inevitably connected with Christ, or as being the place to find Christ, is nothing better than to go back to the beggarly elements of the old Romish harlot, instead of standing in the "liberty wherewith Christ hath made us free," and bidding the sinner to come as a sinner to Christ Jesus, and to Christ Jesus alone.[28]

The Importance of Regeneration

Spurgeon's passionate commitment to baptistic theology was part and parcel of his commitment to the importance of the new birth and faith in Christ. He wanted others to do as he had done: to look with simple faith to Christ alone and find themselves born again. And between baptism and regeneration, the latter, he was clear, was far and away the more vital necessity. "We would do a great deal to make a Paedo-baptist brother into a Baptist," he once said, "but, at the same time, our grand object is not the revision of opinions, but the regeneration of natures."[29]

Regeneration was one of the "three Rs" (ruin, redemption, and regeneration) he always sought to preach. "They contain the sum and substance

---

[26] *MTP*, 10:325. "Puseyism" is a reference to the views of Professor E. B. Pusey of Oxford University, one of the leading lights of the Oxford Movement, which developed and popularized Anglo-Catholicism in the nineteenth century.
[27] *MTP*, 10:413–24.
[28] *MTP*, 10:421.
[29] C. H. Spurgeon, *The Soul Winner: How to Lead Sinners to the Saviour* (New York: Fleming H. Revell, 1895), 10.

of divinity."[30] And regeneration was something he always *expected* to see as he preached the gospel. A friend of his once came to him, depressed because for three months of ministry he had not seen a single conversion. Spurgeon slyly asked, "Do you expect the Lord to save souls every time you open your mouth?" Embarrassed, the man answered "Oh, no, sir!" "Then," Spurgeon replied, "that is just the reason why you have not had conversions: 'According to your faith be it unto you.'"[31]

Regeneration starts the Christian life, and it defines the Christian life. As such, it operated as a fundamental, governing principle in Spurgeon's theology, shaping how he lived, how he preached, and how he saw people. Take, for example, this striking and touching vignette from "Covenant Blessings," a sermon we will examine in more detail in the next chapter:

> Bring hither the poorest peasant; let her if you will be an aged woman, wrinkled and haggard with labour and with years; let her be ignorant of all learning; but, let me know that in her there is faith in Christ, and that consequently the Holy Ghost dwells in her; I will reverence her above all emperors and kings, for she is above them. What are these crowned ones but men who, perhaps, have waded through slaughter to a throne, while she has been uplifted by the righteousness of Jesus. Their dynasty is, after all, of mushroom growth, but she is of the blood royal of the skies. She hath God within her; Christ is waiting to receive her into his bliss; heaven's inhabitants without her could not be perfected, nor God's purpose be fulfilled, therefore is she noblest of the noble. Judge not after the sight of the eyes, but judge ye after the mind of God, and let saved sinners be precious in your sight.[32]

Above any natural or social identity, the new birth gives believers a royal and heavenly identity wholly unconnected to their performance. Peasant girls become princesses, the villainous are made righteous, and a poor country boy from Essex became "above all emperors and kings": for a vice-ridden and classist city like nineteenth-century London, it was transformative theology—as it is still today.

---

[30] *NPSP*, 1:114.
[31] *Autobiog.*, 2:151.
[32] *MTP*, 18:228.

CHAPTER 6

HUMAN SIN AND
GOD'S GRACE

The Problem of Sin

The fact that Spurgeon considered regeneration so important and necessary is revealing of just how deep a view of sin he had. If sin merely weakened us, we would hardly need so radical a solution as new birth: a small leg up would do us fine. Spurgeon held, with the apostle Paul, that unbelieving sinners are spiritually dead in their sins (Eph. 2:1). And, he maintained, that is even worse than it sounds. We naturally assume that that "deadness" equates to simple corpse-like spiritual inertia. In fact, it involves an active *hostility* to God (Rom. 8:7). Thus, when preaching on Colossians 3:17—"whatever you do, in word or deed, do everything in the name of the Lord Jesus"—he was unequivocal in explaining that no unbeliever could possibly obey this. "Until your nature is renewed . . . you are not capable of walking after this high and hallowed fashion. 'Ye must be born again.'"[1]

The reason for this innate inability to please or be pleased with God is simple, he believed: far deeper than any fault in our *behavior*, we are all born with a thorough perversion in the very root of our *being*. "The root must be changed before the fruit can be bettered."[2] Following Ephesians 2:1–3, Spurgeon understood our "deadness" to involve living in "the *passions* of our flesh, carrying out the *desires* of the body and the mind." The

---

[1] *MTP*, 16:62.
[2] *MTP*, 16:62.

problem, in other words, is not that we are born spiritually *weak* but that "in our hearts there is an *aversion* to Christ."[3] The desires of our hearts, which should incline us *to* Christ, incline sinners *away* from him to anything else. Sin is a congenital heart-malady or raving dementia in which we "put bitter for sweet and sweet for bitter, darkness for light and light for darkness."[4] With that basic orientation shaping our very being, we naturally find ourselves (for all our protestations to the contrary) *desiring* sin, self, and darkness while *detesting* God and true righteousness. As such, while we may live lives of outward morality and even charity, we are born enemies of God who cannot even *want* rightly.

With our hearts in that condition, there is no possibility that we might ever trust the God we have such a distaste for. And therein lies our slavery and the essential nature of our sin: the desires of our sinful hearts keep us from faith more effectively than any chains. Worse than misbehavior, by ourselves we cannot and we will not trust God.

> I feel that, could we roll all sins into one mass,—could we take murder, blasphemy, lust, adultery, fornication, and everything that is vile, and unite them all into one vast globe of black corruption,—they would not even then equal the sin of unbelief. This is the monarch sin, the quintessence of guilt, the mixture of the venom of all crimes, the dregs of the wine of Gomorrah; it is the A1 sin, the masterpiece of Satan, the chief work of the devil.[5]

It all had to affect the way Spurgeon pastored. He knew that unbelievers are not impartial seekers after the truth; they cannot therefore be converted through simple rationalism. He was, for example, politely critical of Robert Redford's *The Christian's Plea against Modern Unbelief* in its attempt to create among skeptics an intellectual neutrality toward theism. As Spurgeon saw it, there is no such thing as neutrality. The unbelieving heart is hostile to God and is not brought nearer to faith by the adoption of theism over agnosticism or atheism. The monotheist Muslim is no nearer to saving faith than the polytheist Hindu or the atheist philosopher. Attempts to win people to a Christless "simple theism" as a staging post for saving faith were, he believed, like trying to solve crime by "intreating burglars not to

---

[3] *MTP*, 34:555–56, my emphasis.
[4] *MTP*, 17:385.
[5] *Autobiog.*, 1:261.

carry fire-arms."[6] Not only heads but hearts and desires must be engaged and won.

> A sinner has a heart as well as a head; a sinner has emotions as well as thoughts; and we must appeal to both. A sinner will never be converted until his emotions are stirred. Unless he feels sorrow for sin, and unless he has some measure of joy in the reception of the Word, you cannot have much hope of him. The Truth must soak into the soul, and dye it with its own colour. The Word must be like a strong wind sweeping through the whole heart, and swaying the whole man, even as a field of ripening corn waves in the summer breeze. Religion without emotion is religion without life.[7]

Not that Spurgeon was advocating mindless emotionalism—or emotional*ism* of any sort, for that matter. He knew full well that a sinner can be moved to smiles, frowns, or floods of tears (even in a sermon) and yet remain spiritually unmoved. Emotions can be fickle and superficial things, and are not infallible indicators of the deeper grain of the heart. Rather, Spurgeon sought to preach that truth which has the power to win and overturn the hearts of the dead at their deepest level. And that truth, of course, is Christ. "If you would preach sinners to Christ you must preach Christ to sinners, for nothing so attracts the hearts of men as Jesus himself. The best argument to bring sinners to believe in Jesus is Jesus."[8]

Also, with such a theology of sin and such an understanding of how people work, Spurgeon could never be a moralist. That would be like attempting "to teach a tiger the virtues of vegetarianism."[9] If a person's behavior is merely the fruit and manifestation of what is going on down in the roots of his or her heart, then it would be entirely muddle-headed to think of trying to alter someone's behavior by itself. It would be like skin grafting to cure leprosy. For the short time that the unbeliever managed to carry off a semblance of Christian behavior, it would all be a sham. And it could not last long in any case. Sooner or later the old lusts would show

---

[6] George C. Needham, *The Life and Labors of Charles H. Spurgeon* (Boston: D. L. Guernsey, 1887), 334–35.

[7] C. H. Spurgeon, *The Soul Winner: How to Lead Sinners to the Saviour* (New York: Fleming H. Revell, 1895), 19–20.

[8] *MTP*, 19:193. "To try to win a soul for Christ by keeping that soul in ignorance of any truth, is contrary to the mind of the Spirit; and to endeavour to save men by mere claptrap, or excitement, or oratorical display, is as foolish as to hope to hold an angel with bird-lime, or lure a star with music. The best attraction is the gospel in its purity" (Spurgeon, *The Soul Winner*, 18).

[9] *ARM*, 322.

themselves, and no amount of resolutions could hold them back. Only if hearts are changed will lives be changed.[10]

Human Inability

On March 7, 1858, Spurgeon preached a sermon titled "Human Inability," on Jesus's words from John 6:44, "No man can come to me, except the Father which hath sent me draw him" (KJV).[11] Early on in his ministry, this sermon staked out a position on human slavery to sin that he would never leave.

First, he explained, the sinner's inability to come to Christ does not come from any physical or mental defect as such: "I can believe this Bible to be true just as easily as I can believe any other book to be true. So far as believing on Christ is an act of the mind, I am just as able to believe on Christ as I am able to believe on anybody else."[12] The unbeliever—like the Devil—can have an intellectual grasp of what sin is, who God is, and so on. The problem is with the *corruption* of the unbeliever's mind and nature: the sinful mind has a gravitational pull toward certain things and not others. Just as it is in the nature of a sheep to want grass and not meat, so it is in the nature of a sinner to want sin and not God. Physically there is no reason why a sheep cannot eat meat or a lion eat grass, but it is against their natures, and in this sense they *cannot* do so.

The problem lies in the obstinacy of the human will. "'Oh!' saith the Arminian, 'men may be saved if they will.' We reply, 'My dear sir, we all believe that; but it is just the *if they will* that is the difficulty.'"[13] Sinners do not naturally *want* Christ, and so they never naturally choose him. Added to this, the sinner's understanding is darkened so that he cannot appreciate the glory of God in the cross, creation, or anything in the gospel. He may know every letter of a catechism and yet be untouched by its spirit. And whence arise these problems?

> Assuredly, dear brethren, we can trace them to no other source than this, the corruption and vitiation of the affections. We love that which we ought to hate, and we hate that which we ought to love. It is but human nature, fallen human nature, that man should love this present life better

---

10 *S&T: 1877*, 73.
11 *NPSP*, 4:137–44.
12 *NPSP*, 4:138.
13 *NPSP*, 4:138.

than the life to come. It is but the effect of the fall, that man should love sin better than righteousness, and the ways of this world better than the ways of God. And again, we repeat it, until these affections be renewed, and turned into a fresh channel by the gracious drawings of the Father, it is not possible for any man to love the Lord Jesus Christ.[14]

And it is not as if we have conscience as an infallible guide to save us here, said Spurgeon. When Adam sinned, *every* human faculty was corrupted, including our conscience. The unenlightened human conscience does not comprehend the seriousness or damnable nature of sin. "In fact," he asks, "did conscience ever bring a man to such a self-renunciation, that he did totally abhor himself and all his works and come to Christ? No, conscience, although it is not dead, is ruined, its power is impaired."[15]

Altogether, then, unwilling sinners are powerless in themselves to come to Christ. Unwilling and unable, sinners are completely culpable and completely impotent as they willingly wallow in their sin. Not even a gospel preacher can, by his own power, draw sinners to Christ. The Father must draw them through his life-giving Spirit, and he does so by turning their desires. "Mark that in the Father's drawing there is no compulsion whatever; Christ never compelled any man to come to him against his will. If a man be unwilling to be saved, Christ does not save him against his will. How, then, does the Holy Spirit draw him? Why, by making him willing."[16]

And how exactly does God make sinners willing? Not by mere argumentation or moral persuasion. "He goes to the secret fountain of the heart" so that we become "glad to obey the voice which once we had despised."[17] God enlightens us to appreciate both our wretched state and his glory and grace, and makes us willing and able to come to Christ.

How Grace Triumphs

As Spurgeon saw it, the new birth of a Christian has to be a work of pure divine grace: the sinful human heart is impotent, unwilling, and wholly unworthy. In fact, he declared, God's work of new creation is even more glorious than his original work of creation. After all, more than having to create out of nothing, in regenerating hearts God must overturn that which

---

14 *NPSP*, 4:139.
15 *NPSP*, 4:140.
16 *NPSP*, 4:142.
17 *NPSP*, 4:142.

is overtly hostile to himself. Therefore, Spurgeon said, "I believe the Eternal might sooner forgive the sin of ascribing the creation of the heavens and the earth to an idol, than that of ascribing the works of grace to the efforts of the flesh, or to anyone but himself."[18]

This provided him with great pastoral comfort as he worked amid all the mass degradation of working-class London. It meant that he was not left supposing that there are some more able and some so dehumanized as to be beyond hope. Rather, because regeneration is a matter of God's grace and not human worthiness, "there is no indifference so callous, no ignorance so blind, no iniquity so base, no conscience so seared as not to be made to yield, when God wills it, before the might of His strength."[19] When the Father sends his Spirit to open blind eyes to the glories of Christ and to melt proud hearts, then hearts will indeed be won, and hatred for God turned to love.

The means God uses are his own Word and truth. As such, the

> sermons that are most likely to convert people seem to me to be those that are full of truth, truth about the fall, truth about the law, truth about human nature, and its alienation from God, truth about Jesus Christ, truth about the Holy Spirit, truth about the Everlasting Father, truth about the new birth, truth about obedience to God, and how we learn it, and all such great verities.[20]

Yet, while God uses his truth, his final object is not the head but the heart. Through his Word he enlightens minds *in order that* hearts might be healed and won to himself. Preachers, therefore, must avoid vacuousness in their preaching, and they must avoid heartless intellectualism. The object of all true preaching, after all, is the heart, and preaching has failed "unless it makes men tremble, makes them sad, and then anon brings them to Christ, and causes them to rejoice. Sermons are to be heard in thousands, and yet how little comes of them all, because the heart is not aimed at, or else the archers miss the mark."[21]

In particular (and this is worth more unpacking in the next chapter), God uses the truth of Christ crucified to draw all people to himself (John 12:32). At the very beginning of his ministry in London, Spurgeon

---

[18] *MTP*, 44:565.
[19] *Autobiog.*, 3:3.
[20] Spurgeon, *The Soul Winner*, 90–91.
[21] *MTP*, 27:530.

described his own experience of regeneration through the message of the cross. He pictured himself, a few years earlier, as a slave to his sinful passions, like Byron's hapless character Mazeppa, "bound on the wild horse of my lust, bound hand and foot, incapable of resistance."[22] Locked up "in the strong old castle of my sins," he said, he resisted all preachers who came to the gate of his heart and pleaded with him. Then at last came one

> with loving countenance; his hands were marked with scars, where nails were driven, and his feet had nail-prints too; he lifted up his cross, using it as a hammer; at the first blow the gate of my prejudice shook; at the second it trembled more; at the third down it fell, and in he came; and he said, "Arise, and stand upon thy feet, for I have loved thee with an everlasting love."[23]

The cross—that deepest revelation of the glory of God—is the great weapon that breaks down the heart's defenses. Where the good news of Christ crucified is passed over, preaching must lack the power of God to save sinners. The cross is the essential revelation used by the Spirit to humble and transform us. When the Spirit opens our eyes to appreciate the cross, then "that which was sweet becomes bitter; that which was bright becomes dim."[24]

The very first effect of regeneration is that the sinner comes to Christ.[25] After all, it is not simply that the Spirit has healed the heart so that it loves as it was meant to; the sinner has been breathed upon by the Spirit, and the life which the Spirit gives is none other than the life of Christ.[26] The Father's own love for Christ has been awakened, and God's own divine and holy tastes have been implanted. God's very life has come into the human soul, and so the sinner must now believe, and love, and long for holiness and the spread of God's glory.[27]

---

[22] *NPSP*, 1:57.
[23] *NPSP*, 1:58.
[24] *MTP*, 17:378.
[25] *NPSP*, 4:137. For all that Spurgeon esteemed that moment of conversion, he did not want believers putting their trust in the event.

> One person complains to me, "Sir, I cannot tell exactly when I was converted, and this causes me great anxiety." Dear friend, this is a needless fear. Turn your enquiries in another direction,—Are you alive unto God by faith? Do you believe that Jesus is the Christ, the Son of God? Are you resting and trusting in him? "Yes," say you, "with all my heart." Well, never mind about *when* you were converted; the fact is before you, and its date is a small matter. (*MTP*, 27:662)

[26] *S&T: 1865*, 116.
[27] C. H. Spurgeon, *Memories of Stambourne* (London: Passmore & Alabaster, 1891), 137.

A Wholly New Nature

So far in all this, Spurgeon has simply been articulating a conventional Reformed understanding of sin and regeneration. Yet, in order to underline human inability and God's grace, he also developed a more peculiar opinion with greater similarities (almost certainly wholly unintended) to the theology of Irenaeus of Lyons. As Spurgeon saw it, man naturally consists only of a body and soul, but when he is regenerated, there is created in him a third and *wholly new* nature: the spirit. This is a higher nature, beyond anything in creation; it is a *super*natural, heavenly, and immortal nature "which is a spark from the everlasting fire of God's life and love; this falls into the heart and abides there and makes its receiver 'a partaker of the divine nature' [cf. 2 Pet. 1:4]."[28] Regeneration thus does something more than make a sinner spiritually alive; "its essence lies in the implantation and creation of a new principle within the man."[29]

To explain, Spurgeon elaborated on Paul's comments on the resurrection body in 1 Corinthians 15:44–47: "If there is a natural body, there is also a spiritual body. Thus it is written, 'The first man Adam became a living being'; the last Adam became a life-giving spirit. But it is not the spiritual that is first but the natural, and then the spiritual." We have all been born, he explained, in the natural or "soulish" stage of being, like the first Adam. Then, in regeneration, the Spirit implants in us a new and higher nature, and we become possessors of the life-giving "spirit." Thus, through the new birth, humanity is brought to a higher state than it had ever known before, even in Eden. "What was man in Eden compared with man in Christ? In Paradise he was perfect in beauty, but in Jesus he wears a radiance superlative, for the Holy Ghost is within him. In Adam man was made a living soul, but in Christ Jesus he has now risen to the dignity and majesty of a quickening spirit."[30] Christians can thus be seen to be beyond and above other people, possessing a nature no other human has. Where others are "soulish" and duplex, having only body and soul, Christians are of a "spiritual" and triple nature: spirit, soul, and body.[31]

It certainly served to reinforce the incapacity of the sinner. No humans could grow themselves such a nature, and no preacher could form it in his hearers. Such a spiritual nature must be the gift of God. Yet is this *re-*

---

[28] *S&T: 1879*, 153.
[29] Spurgeon, *The Soul Winner*, 23.
[30] *MTP*, 18:225.
[31] *MTP*, 17:383.

demption? On Spurgeon's account here, the new creation is not about the redemption of God's original handiwork; it is the addition of something *on top of it*. Indeed, Spurgeon was quite clear: "When the Lord new creates us, he borrows nothing from the old man, but makes all things new. He does not repair."[32] Rather, in regeneration, God builds a whole new temple "rising to something better."[33] To be sure, we gain more in Christ than ever we lost in Adam, but Spurgeon seems to overstate his case here, temporarily losing something of the *restorative* and *reconciliatory* aspects of salvation.[34]

Covenant Blessings

Spurgeon's overall understanding of regeneration is neatly encapsulated in a sermon he preached on Ezekiel 36:26–27, titled "Covenant Blessings."[35] Given shortly after a time of personal spiritual depression, it was meant to encourage those struggling with assurance.

The Spirit's first work in us, he explained, is to remove the old heart and give a new one (that is, "to pull down the old house and build himself a new one"). "A new heart is absolutely essential, we must be born again or the Spirit of truth cannot abide within us."[36] This is in direct opposition to how we seek to improve ourselves. We work at our behavior and external things in the hope that outside changes will affect us on the inside and make us better people all through. "God's way of dealing with men is the reverse. He begins within and works towards the exterior in due course."[37] And this is how it must be with a deep-seated problem like sin. Polishing the outside and tinkering with externals can do nothing to cure the inner source and spring of all our corruption, which is the heart. In particular, the gift of a "new heart" means the radical transformation of our affections and desires. "The affections are the most powerful part of our nature, they to a great extent mould even the understanding itself, and if the heart be defiled all the mental faculties become disturbed in their balance. God, therefore, commences at the heart."[38] With such a new heart, the believer "receives new inspirations, feeds on new food, longs for new happiness,

---

[32] *MTP*, 17:377.
[33] *MTP*, 17:383.
[34] For a more detailed (and fiery) critique of such "third nature" theology, see Abraham Kuyper, *The Work of the Holy Spirit* (Grand Rapids: Eerdmans, 1946), 331–32.
[35] *MTP*, 18:217–28.
[36] *MTP*, 18:219.
[37] *MTP*, 18:219.
[38] *MTP*, 18:220.

performs new actions, and is, in fact, an inhabitant of the new heavens and the new earth wherein dwelleth righteousness."[39]

The second covenant blessing mentioned by Ezekiel is the gift of a new spirit. As we might now expect, Spurgeon saw this as something *additional* to the gift of the new heart.

> It is our own belief that in regeneration something more is done than the mere rectifying of what was there: there is in the new birth infused and implanted in man a third and more elevated principle,—a spirit is begotten in him; and, as the second Adam was made a quickening spirit, so in the new birth we are transformed into the likeness of Christ Jesus, who is the second Adam.[40]

Where the natural man lives all for himself and only dreads God, the spiritual new man has different motivations, different fears and different pleasures. God is his beloved Father, and the new man loves to please him. He now hates sin, and not (as once he had) for the thought of its punishment, but for its own foulness and offensiveness to God. "It is a revolution indeed, when the hatred and dread of a slave are exchanged for the loving subjection of a son."[41]

The third blessing Ezekiel pronounces is the removal of the stony heart. This does not mean that in the act of regeneration the Lord immediately removes all sinful desires; it is rather that the stony *hardness* of the heart is undone. God melts our cold insensibility to himself.

At this point in the sermon, Spurgeon made a helpful observation about the relationship between the heart's *affections* and our *emotions*. While related and interconnected, the two are not the same thing. The affections make up the essential grain and orientation of the heart; they are not to be confused with emotions which come and go according to circumstance. Thus preachers must not fall into the trap of imagining that they are transforming deep *affections* when they are simply manipulating passing *emotions*.

> I know preachers who delight in talking of a mother's tears, and a father's grey hairs, of dying children and consumptive sisters, and I believe these are all legitimate topics; but, no hearts are ever turned from stone to flesh

---

[39] *MTP*, 18:220.
[40] *MTP*, 18:221.
[41] *MTP*, 18:221.

merely by natural emotion. You may make a man weep over his dead child or his dead wife, till his eyes are red, but his heart will be black for all that.[42]

The fourth blessing Spurgeon observed in Ezekiel is the gift of a heart of flesh. Where once we had hearts that were unfeeling and unyielding toward God and righteousness, God has given Christians "a heart which can feel, can be moved to shame, to repentance, to loathing of sin, to desiring, to seeking, to panting, to longing after God."[43] With such a heart, the sinner will cry out in true repentance for the first time, asking for forgiveness and wanting to know the presence of God.

Here again Spurgeon inserted a helpful pastoral lesson. We must not mistake natural tenderness for this "heart of flesh." Some people are born *constitutionally* sensitive, but that does not mean they are *spiritually* sensitive. It may well be that they are simply impressionable and can be influenced quickly for evil as well as good. Thus they can appear affected by the things of the gospel when it is only a matter of circumstance: place them in a mosque or a bar and they would be equally affected. Mere impressibility is not grace. "Beware, then, that you do not mistake the gilding of nature for the solid gold of grace."[44]

With that, Spurgeon turned to the despairing listener who felt "My heart is so bad, so hard, so cold, I can believe in Christ but I cannot change my nature." Spurgeon answered, "Poor soul, there is no need you should, for there is one who can do the work for you."[45] Regeneration is a work of pure grace—and those the Lord regenerates, he will indwell. And "with such an indweller we need not fear, but that this poor heart of ours will yet become perfect as God is perfect; and our nature through his indwelling shall rise into complete meetness for the inheritance of the saints in light."[46] Those the Lord renews internally he will purify—and ultimately glorify—all through.

---

42 *MTP*, 18:222.
43 *MTP*, 18:222–23.
44 *MTP*, 18:224.
45 *MTP*, 18:224.
46 *MTP*, 18:225.

CHAPTER 7

THE CROSS AND NEW BIRTH

The Centrality of the Cross

It is only right that a chapter on the cross should stand at the center of this book, for the cross stood at the center of Spurgeon's own Christian life and ministry, as well as his understanding of the person of Christ and of the Christian life itself. In fact, the rest of this book would be downright misleading without this chapter, for the cross was the axle in Spurgeon's theology.

In the end, all talk of the centrality of Christ would, for Spurgeon, be inaccurate if we separated Christ from his work and failed to mention his crucifixion. "Some may continually preach Christ as an example, and others may perpetually discourse upon his coming to glory: we also preach both of these, but mainly we preach Christ *crucified*."[1] The cross is the pinnacle of Christ's work and the clearest window into his identity: it was the key and the plumb line for Spurgeon as he contemplated Christ and the new life he offers. It also had to be the fulcrum of Spurgeon's gospel if he was to be centered upon the Christ of the Bible who came to make atonement. "To attempt to preach Christ without His cross, is to betray Him with a kiss."[2] Just as Leviticus teaches that the life of the creature is in its blood (Lev. 17:11, 14), so Spurgeon saw that the life of the gospel is found in the blood of Jesus. Without blood it is lifeless.[3] "Those men who take away the

---

[1] *MTP*, 33:374.
[2] *ARM*, 365.
[3] *MTP*, 34:111.

atonement from the gospel murder the gospel; they are like vampires, that suck the blood out of the living man's veins, and lay him dead."[4]

Practically, it meant that he insisted upon celebrating Christ's death in the Lord's Supper every Lord's Day, and often broke bread during the week as well.[5] And "celebrating," he believed, was the right word: "The bread and the cup . . . evoke no tears, they suggest no sighs. The memorial of Christ's death is a festival, not a funeral; and we are to come to the table with gladsome hearts."[6] And it meant that he preached on Christ crucified so frequently, it became known as his heart theme. "Dear friends, I am going to preach to you again upon the corner-stone of the gospel," he once announced from the pulpit. "How many times will this make, I wonder? The doctrine of Christ crucified is always with me."[7] Moreover, the cross provided Spurgeon with a focal point that determined for him where issues of life or doctrine belong in order of prominence. "More and more," he told his students, "am I jealous lest any views upon prophecy, church government, politics, or even systematic theology, should withdraw one of us from glorying in the cross of Christ."[8]

The cross, as Spurgeon put it, is Christ's throne of grace and the central act of redemption typified in the Old Testament by all the sacrifices of the law and the redemptions of God's people. It is the apparently foolish wisdom of God which saves the simple and the children, and which humbles the educated and the proud. It makes the gospel for common people rather than an elite of any sort. "The most educated must find their wisdom in the cross, or die fools."[9] It is the tree of life, the ladder to heaven, and the crux of true logic.

> All good things lie within the compass of the cross; its outstretched arms overshadow the whole world of thought; from the east even unto the west it sheds a hallowed influence; meanwhile, its foot is planted deep in the eternal mysteries, and its top pierces all earth-born clouds, and rises to the throne of the Most High.[10]

The cross being so pivotal, Spurgeon made it the emblem of his Pastors' College, surrounding it with the motto *Et Teneo Et Teneor*, "I Hold and Am

---

4 *MTP*, 57:533.
5 *MTP*, 33:376.
6 *MTP*, 38:139.
7 *MTP*, 33:374.
8 *Lectures*, 1:83.
9 *MTP*, 32:416.
10 *MTP*, 33:376.

Figure 2

ET TENEO   ET TENEOR.

"I HOLD"   & AM HELD."

Held" (fig. 2): "I hold" because Christ crucified is the saving and sanctifying truth we must hold out to all people; "I am held" because the blood of Christ is what attracts us to Christ and what holds us safe in Christ. "We labour to hold forth the cross of Christ with a bold hand among the sons of men, because that cross holds us fast by its attractive power."[11]

One word of clarification is in order here: for Spurgeon, the cross-work of Christ is *central*, but it is absolutely *inseparable* from the rest of his work. "The cross" cannot be considered in abstraction or isolation from the person of Christ or his life, resurrection, ascension, and so forth.

> There has risen up a modern idea which I cannot too much reprobate, that Christ made no atonement for our sin except upon the cross: whereas in this passage of Isaiah we are taught as plainly as possible that by his bruising and his stripes, as well as by his death, we are healed. Never divide between the life and the death of Christ. How could he have died if he had not lived? How could he suffer except while he lived? Death is not suffering, but the end of it. Guard also against the evil notion that you have nothing to do with the righteousness of Christ, for he could not have made an atonement by his blood if he had not been perfect in his life. He could not have been acceptable if he had not first been proven to be holy, harmless, and undefiled. The victim must be spotless, or it cannot be presented for sacrifice. Draw no nice lines and raise no quibbling questions, but look at your Lord as he is and bow before him.[12]

[11] *Autobiog.*, 2:150.
[12] *MTP*, 25:426.

As Christ's holy life and active righteousness are as essential to our salvation as his death and passive righteousness, so we must not imagine that
the cross alone equals the full work of salvation. Spurgeon *would* preach the
birth, life, resurrection, and ascension of Christ. The cross remained central, but for him to ignore those other facets of redemption would have distorted his gospel just as if he had built his message on another cornerstone.

It is not quite enough, though, to speak of the *centrality* of the cross
for Spurgeon. He also wanted to speak of its *preeminence*. The cross stands
preeminent among all the mighty works of God and must be held out pre-
eminently. What this means he illustrated in a revealing and quite unusual
aside during one of his sermons. It was unusual in that it took issue with
one of the details in his greatly beloved *Pilgrim's Progress*. In the aside he
told the story of a young missionary in Edinburgh, Scotland, who got a
shock when, using Bunyan's language, he asked a woman there if she was
carrying a spiritual burden on her back:

> "What!" she said; "do you mean that burden in John Bunyan's 'Pilgrim's Prog-
> ress?' Because if you do, young man, I have got rid of that many years ago,
> before you were born. But I went a better way to work than the pilgrim did.
> The evangelist that John Bunyan talks about was one of your parsons that do
> not preach the Gospel; for he said, 'Keep that light in thine eye and run to
> the wicket-gate.' Why, man alive! that was not the place for him to run to. He
> should have said, 'Do you see that cross? Run there at once!' But instead of
> that, he sent the poor pilgrim to the wicket-gate first; and much good he got
> by going there!—he got tumbling into the slough, and was like to have been
> killed by it." "But did you," he asked, "go through any slough of despond?"
> "Yes, young man, I did; but I found it a great deal easier going through with my
> burden off, than with it on my back." The old woman was quite right. We must
> not say to the sinner, "Now, sinner, if thou wilt be saved go to the baptismal
> pool—go to the wicket-gate—go to the church—do this or that." No, the cross
> should be right in front of the wicket-gate, and we should say to the sinner,
> "Throw thyself there, and thou art safe. But thou art not safe till thou canst
> cast off thy burden, and lie at the foot of the cross, and find peace in Jesus."[13]

Before and above all, the message sinners need to hear is the message of
Christ crucified. That is what will supremely "draw all people" to Christ
(John 12:32), kill sin, and turn hearts of stone into hearts of flesh.

---

[13] *MTP*, 58:599.

The Cross Mortifies

The cross is also *foremost* for Spurgeon in that it shapes the believer's first experience of salvation. Those who enjoy new life in Christ are said to have been crucified with him already (Rom. 6:1–8). In the experience of the new birth there is a death to be endured before there is a coming to life.

Spurgeon elaborated on this in a sermon preached in 1871 on Isaiah 40:6–7:

> All flesh is grass,
>> and all its beauty is like the flower of the field.
> The grass withers, the flower fades
>> when the breath of the LORD blows on it.[14]

"There is," he explained, "a withering wrought by the Spirit which is the preparation for the sowing and implanting by which salvation is wrought."[15] Before this, we blithely suppose ourselves to be rather nice and pleasant— or, at the very least, that we deserve to be in the right with God and men. What awareness we have of our faults is superficial and excused. "We confess that we may have committed faults, but we think them very venial, and we venture, in our wicked pride, to imagine that, after all, we are not so vile as the word of God would lead us to think."[16] Then the Spirit opens our eyes to see ourselves for what we truly are: not beautiful and lovely but wretched in our pride, selfishness, and slavery to evil. He thus humbles us by sharing with us his own disgust at sin and letting us feel the justice of his sentence of death upon us. We find ourselves shocked and horrified at what we are.

This first work of grace in the sinner is a pulling down of the old man and a demolition of his vaunting and deluded self-confidence and self-love. The Holy Spirit "will come as the fire, and cause a conflagration of all proud nature's Babels."[17] That all sounds odious to a culture of self-esteem, but it is a work of real divine kindness. All my natural avoidance of guilt—all the blame shifting and excuses—is ended by the Spirit's illumination, and it is ended *so that* the guilt can be faced and resolved. It is the divine surgeon's painful but necessary operation. Instead of callously ignoring our inner

---

14 *MTP*, 17:373–84.
15 *MTP*, 17:374.
16 *MTP*, 17:379.
17 *MTP*, 17:376.

corruption, he opens us up to remove it. It is the stripping before we can be clothed with real beauty and righteousness. It is the enlightenment that makes us see our need for cleansing.

And it must hurt. Sinners will turn away from the dark habits and temptations that had previously charmed them only if they feel "*a very deep and poignant sorrow on account of sin.*"[18] If their pride, lust, and selfishness do not distress them, they will not declare war on them. Without sorrow for sin, they would not have the heartbeat of the new life in Christ or a share in the mind of the Spirit. "We cannot conceive it possible that you are broken in heart if the pleasures of the world are your delight."[19] And it is not only sorrow for sin that hurts: this "withering" of the Spirit is painful because just at the point where the sinner begins to feel the foul truth about his sin he feels himself utterly unable to get rid of it.

> He who believes himself able to save himself has never known the meaning of a broken heart. Those who imagine that reformation can atone for the past, or secure righteousness for the future, are not yet savingly brought to know themselves. No, my friends, we must be humbled in the dust, and made to look for all in Christ, or else we shall be deceived after all.[20]

Those whom the Spirit withers will feel helpless, like wounded soldiers crying out to be carried to a hospital. They are driven out of themselves that they might trust only in Christ and not on themselves anymore.

Since this mortification throws people onto Christ for deliverance, it is *temporarily* painful work that ultimately produces a richer, sturdier Christian happiness.

> This is mournful work, but it must be done. I think those who experience much of it when they first come to Christ have great reason to be thankful. Their course in life will, in all probability, be much brighter and happier, for I have noticed that persons who are converted very easily, and come to Christ with but comparatively little knowledge of their own depravity, have to learn it afterwards, and they remain for a long time babes in Christ, and are perplexed with matters that would not have troubled them if they had experienced a deeper work at first.[21]

---

18 *NPSP*, 1:406.
19 *NPSP*, 1:406.
20 *NPSP*, 1:407.
21 *MTP*, 17:381.

Spurgeon knew that every conversion story is different and unique. Some experience this stage of mortification far more acutely than others. Some hardly experience it at all. "Any true conversion is good, but we confess our liking to the old-fashioned Bunyan-like experience. A little drenching and half-drowning in terror nauseates men of iniquity, and this is a great point gained."[22] John Bunyan had, like Spurgeon himself, gone through years of depression and self-despair before trusting and finding comfort in Christ. It was an invaluable experience (recorded in his *Grace Abounding to the Chief of Sinners*) which kept him as a Christian from self-reliance. The Spirit had mortified him so that he could enjoy the new life that is to be had in Christ. "We have not all endured the ordeal so long, but in every child of God there must be a death to sin, to the law, and to self, which must be fully accomplished ere he is perfected in Christ and taken to heaven."[23]

The Cross Vivifies

The cross must also be held preeminent because, as well as mortifying proud sinners, it is God's means of bringing them to new life. Normally that works as follows. First, the sinner realizes his sin and despairs of himself.

> Then, comes the Holy Spirit and shows the sinner the cross of Christ, gives him eyes anointed with heavenly eye-salve, and says, "Look to yonder cross, that Man died to save sinners; you feel that you are a sinner; he died to save you." And he enables the heart to believe, and to come to Christ.[24]

Yet, though Spurgeon believed that was the *normal* process of conversion, he was wary of being overly prescriptive. Christ (and especially Christ crucified) draws people to himself by his own appeal, and this may not always involve that preliminary stage of mortification.

> Among the many thousands of souls who have been brought to know the Lord under my instrumentality, I have often noticed that a considerable proportion of these, and of the best members of our church, too, were won to the Saviour, not by legal terrors, but by gentler means. Sitting,

---

[22] *S&T: 1883*, 29.
[23] *MTP*, 17:380.
[24] *NPSP*, 4:143.

on one occasion, to see enquirers, I should think that there were as
many as twelve out of the twenty-three whose convictions of sin were
not distinctly marked with the terrors of the law. I asked an excellent
young woman, "What was the first thought that set you really seeking the
Saviour?" "Oh, sir!" she replied, "it was Christ's lovely character that first
made me long to be His disciple. I saw how kind, how good, how disinter-
ested, how self-sacrificing He was, and that made me feel how different I
was. I thought, 'Oh! I am not like Jesus!' and that sent me to my room, and
I began to pray, and so I came to trust in Him." "The first religious impression I ever had," said another, "that set me seeking the Saviour, was this; a
young companion of mine fell into sin, and I knew that I was likely to do
the same if I was not kept by someone stronger than myself. I therefore
sought the Lord, not so much at first on account of past transgression, but
because I was afraid of some great future sin. God visited me, and I then
felt conviction of sin, and was brought to Christ." Singularly enough, too, I
have met with scores of persons who have trusted in Christ, and then have
mourned their sins more afterwards than they did before they believed.
Their convictions have been more terrible after they have known their
interest in Christ than they were at first. They have seen the enormity
of the evil after they have escaped from it; they have been plucked out
of the miry clay, and their feet set upon the rock; and then, afterwards,
they have seen more fully the depth of that horrible pit out of which they
have been snatched. . . . There are some who, like Lydia, have their hearts
opened [Acts 16:14], not by the crowbar of conviction, but by the picklock
of Divine grace. Sweetly drawn, almost silently enchanted by the loveli-
ness of Jesus, they say, "Draw me, we will run after Thee [Song 1:4]."[25]

However God exactly brings each sinner to himself, it is Christ (and
especially Christ crucified) who is the magnet. In fact, he is the *only* magnet God ever uses. "I do believe that we slander Christ when we think that
we are to draw the people by something else but the preaching of Christ
crucified."[26] Stirring oratory, soaring music, learned philosophy, and clever
arguments: none have the power to stir the deep affections of human hearts
like a faithful exhibition of Jesus crucified.[27]

This, Spurgeon was adamant, was the only reason why such great
crowds were drawn to his church for so many years. There was nothing

25 *Autobiog.*, 4:29–30.
26 *MTP*, 39:596.
27 See C. H. Spurgeon, *The Saint and His Savior: The Progress of the Soul in the Knowledge of Jesus* (New York: Sheldon, Blakeman & Co., 1858), 149; *MTP*, 16:283.

else to attract them: no especially beautiful architecture, ritual, or music; no elaborate oratory or learned discourse. Services were bare, but Christ crucified was preached, and that was why so many came and why their lives were transformed. That too, he found, had been the testimony of the church's missionaries sent abroad. When they taught on God's existence, greatness, and justice, as well as on sin and its punishment, there was normally no fruit. Only when they began to speak of Christ coming into the world to bear our sins in his death would listless listeners stir and sit up. Across the world, the message that Spurgeon saw touching and overturning hearts at the deepest level was always the message of Jesus's crucifixion.

> Christ crucified is the conqueror. Not in his robes of glory does he subdue the heart, but in his vestments of shame. Not as sitting upon the throne does he at first gain the faith and the affections of sinners, but as bleeding, suffering, and dying in their stead. "God forbid that I should glory," said the apostle, "save in the cross of our Lord Jesus Christ"; and though every theme that is connected with the Saviour ought to play its part in our ministry, yet this is the master theme. The atoning work of Jesus is the great gun of our battery. The cross is the mighty battering-ram wherewith to break in pieces the brazen gates of human prejudices and the iron bars of obstinacy. Christ coming to be our judge alarms, but Christ the man of sorrows subdues. The crown of thorns has a royal power in it to compel a willing allegiance, the sceptre of reed breaks hearts better than a rod of iron, and the robe of mockery commands more love than Cæsar's imperial purple.[28]

Spurgeon felt all this so strongly and thoroughly that he liked to tell the story of the time he visited the Crystal Palace in 1857. He was due to preach at an extraordinary prayer meeting there, which nearly twenty-four thousand people would attend. Anticipating the vocal challenge this would present him, he decided to test the acoustic properties of the building beforehand. Assuming his place, he boomed, "Behold the Lamb of God, which taketh away the sin of the world!" Up in one of the galleries, an unsuspecting workman heard the words and was immediately convicted of his sin. He put down his tools, went home, and (Spurgeon found out later) "found peace and life by beholding the Lamb of God."[29]

---

[28] *MTP*, 23:271.
[29] *Autobiog.*, 2:239.

This being the case, Spurgeon sought (and taught his students) first and foremost to preach Christ and him crucified. Doing that in a rounded and accurate manner did not normally mean simply repeating the words of John 1:29. "The Christian minister," he told his students, "should preach *all* the truths which cluster around the person and work of the Lord Jesus."[30] It meant declaring the evil of sin and the certainty of punishment as well as explaining the mechanics of atonement.

The cross is the message that brings the dead to life, but Spurgeon also saw it as the message that enlivens *all*—even the spiritually sluggish. Christians who wanted to grow in holiness and Christians who had grown apathetic, unbelievers and those unsure about their spiritual state—*all* would be directed to the cross for their change of heart. For example, one doubting believer wrote to him these plaintive words:

> Dear Sir,
>
> Will you be kind enough candidly to inform me whether I have any room for hope that I belong to the elect family of God, whether Jesus Christ His Son has died for me, while my affections are in the world? I try to pray, but cannot. I make resolutions only to break them. I from time to time listen to you when you speak of the glory set apart for the saints, when you describe their joys and their feelings, but I feel myself as having nothing to do with them. O sir, that Sunday morning when you spoke of the hypocrite, I felt that you described me! I go to chapel to hear the Word preached, I return home, and make resolutions; I go to work, then out into the world, and forget all until the time for preaching comes again. I read the Bible, but do not feel interested; it seems no more to me than a book I have before read,—dry and insipid. Christ has said that, of all who come to Him, He will not send any away. How am I to come? I feel that I cannot come. I would if I could, but I cannot. At times, I think that I will give it all up, that I will not go to chapel any more; yet when the time comes, I cannot stay away, but feel compelled to go again once more. Do, dear sir, tell me, how am I to find Jesus? How am I to know that He died for me, and that I belong to His family? Dear sir, tell me, am I a hypocrite?
>
> I remain,
>   Dear sir,
>   Yours to serve in anxiety,
>   T. W. MEDHURST.

---

30 *Lectures*, 2:266–67, my emphasis.

Spurgeon replied by changing the question. The question to ask, he explained, was not "Am I one of God's elect?" but "Am I a sinner?" "Now, if you are such a sinner," he wrote, "I am glad to be able to tell you the only way of salvation, 'Believe on the Lord Jesus.'" Rather than having the doubter look to his own state and wonder, Spurgeon advised him to look *outside* himself—to Christ on the cross. Only out there in Christ could heart-change and solid comfort be found. Thus, Spurgeon concluded his letter:

> There is the cross, and a bleeding God-man upon it; look to Him, and be saved! There is the Holy Spirit able to give you every grace. Look, in prayer, to the Sacred Three-one God, and then you will be delivered.

> I am,
>   Your anxious friend,
>   Write again.
>   C. H. SPURGEON.[31]

The human heart is incapable of reforming itself, and yet in our natural self-dependence we think that mere determination can bring about the deep self-improvement we crave. At such times we rake our performance and our hearts in the hope that we might feel secure in them. Instead, Spurgeon insisted, it is only at the foot of the cross, where our sin and God's judgment and grace are supremely revealed, that we will find a change of heart. Only there is our hope of liberation and purity.[32] There, even the vilest "sinners, who have gone to the very brink of damnation" may "rise to the utmost heights of enthusiastic joy in Jesus." Finding there an entirely undeserved pardon, those who feel their spiritual hardness and inability will experience the transformation they long for. "Put your trust in the Lord Jesus Christ, and all manner of sin and of blasphemy shall be forgiven unto you; and at the receipt of such a pardon you shall burst out into new-made doxologies to God your Saviour."[33]

The Glory of God in the Face of Christ Crucified

Why is it that the message of Jesus's death is so uniquely powerful to enlighten the blind, awaken the dead, and enliven the sluggish Christian?

---

[31] *Autobiog.*, 2:142–44.
[32] *MTP*, 18:227.
[33] *MTP*, 31:240.

Quite simply because in the cross of Christ we see most clearly the glory of God. "For God, who said, 'Let light shine out of darkness,' has shone in our hearts to give the light of the knowledge of the glory of God in the face of Jesus Christ" (2 Cor. 4:6). It is the glory of God that shines light into otherwise impenetrable darkness, and it is by beholding the glory of the Lord that anyone is transformed "from one degree of glory to another" (2 Cor. 3:18).

Spurgeon taught that the minister's "great object of glorifying God" is mainly achieved through the preaching of *"Christ and him crucified."*[34] There the true wisdom, power, holiness, goodness, love, and sovereignty of God are revealed in all their surprising beauty, winning the hearts of those who look to him. And while God is *always* wise, powerful, holy, good, loving, and sovereign, we do not understand or see that aright apart from Christ. His sovereignty, for example, we would mistake for cold tyranny or unfeeling government; his goodness we would take for weak indulgence. Using the imagery of Exodus 33:19–23, understood though Paul's statement in 1 Corinthians 10:4 that "the Rock was Christ," Spurgeon explained:

> Jesus is the clift [*sic*] of the rock wherein we stand when we come to God in Christ Jesus. There it is that we can look upon the goodness and the sovereignty of Jehovah, and more fully survey the glorious vision than it were possible for us to behold anywhere else. *Apart from Christ, men do not see the true goodness of God.* The description that some preachers give of God's goodness amounts to this: that men's sins are such trifles that God will entirely overlook them as frailties of the creature, or if he should punish the transgressors, it will be with gentle discipline, and not with fiery indignation; and that only for a short time, after which they will either perish by annihilation, or else peradventure they will enter into life everlasting by a general restitution. Sin is treated with an indifference that borders on levity. . . .
>
> *Nor does any man ever see God's sovereignty aright until he comes into the clift of the rock, Jesus Christ.* I love the high doctrines of the covenant of grace, I must confess, most devoutly and devotedly. But of this I am quite certain, that all the counsels of the Father concerning his people, and all the benefits he has conferred on his people were bestowed in the person of his well-beloved Son.[35]

---

34 *Lectures*, 2:265–66.
35 *MTP*, 61:102–4.

Could all the perfections or attributes of God's glory be laid out and un-folded before us, we would perceive that "the chief splendour of his Majesty lay in his infinite benevolence. God is love. This is the prominent point of the divine character."[36] And that loving goodness is most fully displayed in God's work of redemption, culminating at the cross.[37] Spurgeon wanted to speak carefully here, knowing he could be misunderstood. In fact, he advised:

> Do not extol the single attribute of love in the method too generally fol-lowed, but regard love in the high theological sense, in which, like a golden circle, it holds within itself all the divine attributes: for God were not love if he were not just, and did not hate every unholy thing. Never exalt one attribute at the expense of another. Let boundless mercy be seen in calm consistency with stern justice and unlimited sovereignty. The true character of God is fitted to awe, impress, and humble the sinner: be careful not to misrepresent your Lord.[38]

When the glory of God is displayed in the cross, we get to see *all* God's perfections. We see that God is not merely helpful to the weak but also long-suffering and infinitely merciful to great sinners. We see the riches of his grace, his sovereign power to save, his holy justice, and his love. And never does one attribute clash with another. "His love does not diminish his justice, nor does his justice, in the least degree, make warfare upon his love. The two things are sweetly linked together in the atonement of Christ."[39] Thus when Spurgeon preached the cross, he sought to witness to the glory of God in all its fullness. Nevertheless, he still thought it right to speak of God's love and grace as "the chief splendour of his Majesty." After all, he would argue, thinking of Ephesians 2:7, "remember that [God] calls his mercy his riches: 'he is rich in mercy.' I do not find that he calls his power his riches, but he calls his grace his riches." Through the cross,

> the Lord, who is rich in mercy, seeks a treasury in which to put his riches; he wants a casket for the sacred jewellery of his love; and these atrocious criminals, these great offenders, these who think themselves black as hell, these are the very men in whom there is space for his rare jewels of goodness.[40]

---

[36] *MTP*, 61:98.
[37] *MTP*, 61:99.
[38] *Lectures*, 2:271.
[39] *NPSP*, 4:132.
[40] *MTP*, 31:236.

And it is especially the love of God shown in the cross that turns and transforms the hearts of sinners. In the horrifying torture and crucifixion of Jesus we see the highest proof of the highest love.[41] His bleeding makes our hearts bleed, and his shame makes us ashamed. In the cross we see a divine disgust at sin that makes sin appalling in our eyes too.[42] But further, through the cross we see a love so livid that it pierces our apathy and overwhelms our desire for other things. Sinners, Spurgeon said, are naturally held back from God by lack of desire for him; "but the cross will breed desire. They are held back by love of sin; but the cross will make them hate the sin that crucified the Saviour."[43] The cross is the quintessence of that love which makes us love (1 John 4:19).

> Who can resist his charms? One look of his eyes overpowers us. See with your heart those eyes when they are full of tears for perishing sinners, and you are a willing subject. One look at his blessed person subjected to scourging and spitting for our sakes will give us more idea of his crown rights than anything besides. Look into his pierced heart as it pours out its life-flood for us, and all disputes about his sovereignty are ended in our hearts. We own him Lord because we see how he loved.[44]

What Happened on the Cross?

So far in this chapter, we have been looking at the cross *as it relates to Spurgeon's theology of the Christian life.* However, left there, it could look as if Spurgeon preached nothing more than a "moral influence" theory of the atonement—Christ merely died to win our hearts. That would be highly misleading. So what exactly did Spurgeon preach when he got to expound on the cross?

Spurgeon believed that on the cross the life-imparting glory of God is revealed and the sin of humanity is exposed. But that is not the primary reason *why* Christ went to the cross. Christ did glorify God and expose sin— but he did so *by atoning for sin.* Only because the cross was an act of atonement was God revealed as a righteous Judge and a loving Savior.

Spurgeon saw a number of different facets to this atonement. He liked to speak of the cross as Jesus's ultimate battle, where sin and death are

---

41 *MTP*, 33:374.
42 *Autobiog.*, 2:226.
43 *MTP*, 39:596.
44 *MTP*, 23:269.

defeated and the Prince of Darkness is driven out. In "Christ Triumphant," for example, he devoted a whole sermon to the theme, describing Jesus as the conquering "victor on the cross," and the cross itself as "Christ's triumphal chariot in which he rode when he led captivity captive."[45] All humanity, he explained, was Satan's slave; then Christ came forth as the deliverer and set us free by defeating and disarming the foe. That means now for Christians that

> Satan has nothing left him now wherewith he may attack us. He may attempt to injure us, but wound us he never can, for his sword and spear are utterly taken away. In the old battles, especially among the Romans, after the enemy had been overcome, it was the custom to take away all their weapons and ammunition; afterwards they were stripped of their armour and their garments, their hands were tied behind their backs, and they were made to pass under the yoke. Now, even so hath Christ done with sin, death, and hell; he hath taken their armour, spoiled them of all their weapons, and made them all to pass under the yoke; so that now they are our slaves, and we in Christ are conquerors of them who were mightier than we.[46]

Yet Spurgeon was no dualist, imagining Satan as a divine rival, equal to God. The defeat of Satan was a wonderful *consequence* of the atonement, but Satan could exist and operate only under the sovereignty of God. Satan could oppress sinners only because God, in his holy fury at sin, permitted him. Before anything else, atonement was needed to deal with *God's* wrath at sin.

At the heart of the cross, then, was a work of penal substitution, and Spurgeon would be both persistent and outspoken in teaching and defending this theme. "All joy is gone from our life if substitution be untrue," he taught.[47] What he meant by penal substitution he made quite clear in "Christ—Our Substitute," a sermon preached early on in his ministry, in 1860:

> The doctrine of Holy Scripture is this, that inasmuch as man could not keep God's law, having fallen in Adam, Christ came and fulfilled the law on the behalf of his people; and that inasmuch as man had already broken the divine law and incurred the penalty of the wrath of God, Christ came

---

45 *NPSP*, 5:385.
46 *NPSP*, 5:388.
47 William Williams, *Personal Reminiscences of Charles Haddon Spurgeon* (London: Passmore & Alabaster, 1895), 167.

and suffered in the room, place, and stead of his elect ones, that so by his enduring the full vials of wrath, they might be emptied out and not a drop might ever fall upon the heads of his blood-bought people.[48]

That is, on the cross Christ "stands in our place, assumes our guilt, takes on him[self] our iniquity, and God treats him as if he had been sin."[49] Christ is our substitute, bearing in our place God's anger at sin and its punishment, death. It meant that in his preaching, Spurgeon liked to hold out to his hearers the joyful exchange between Christ and the sinner:

> He wore my crown, the crown of thorns; I wear his crown, the crown of glory. He wore my dress, nay, rather, he wore my nakedness when he died upon the cross; I wear his robes, the royal robes of the King of kings. He bore my shame; I bear his honour. He endured my sufferings to this end that my joy may be full, and that his joy may be fulfilled in me. He laid in the grave that I might rise from the dead and that I may dwell in him.[50]

Christ's substitutionary sacrifice is essential to the gospel and to faithful preaching, Spurgeon believed. It is the only message which allows—yes, and demands—us to put all our trust in Christ and none in ourselves for salvation. After all, if Christ is our perfect substitute—if our sin is imputed to him and his righteousness to us—then no merit of ours can be necessary. A penal substitutionary atonement means that we can accept by simple faith (and faith alone) what Christ has done for us. It is, then, a soul-saving doctrine of incalculable comfort and joy for believers, and cannot be given up or skewed.

> Cloudy views as to atoning blood are mischievous to the last degree; souls are held in unnecessary bondage, and saints are robbed of the calm confidence of faith, because they are not definitely told that "God hath made Him to be sin for us, who knew no sin, that we might be made the righteousness of God in Him."[51]

More than mischievous, in fact; unorthodox views of the cross and denials of this doctrine Spurgeon saw as blasphemous in how they dishonored

---

48 *NPSP*, 6:191.
49 *NPSP*, 6:194.
50 *NPSP*, 6:195.
51 *Lectures*, 2:269–70.

Christ. For the glory of Christ as well as the comfort of believers, he would defend penal substitution:

> My blood boils that so many men should dare to assail that which the Lord Jehovah has appointed. It was God who devised the plan; it was God who gave his Son out of his own bosom to die; it is God himself who has commended that plan to our hearts, and made us put our trust in his great Sacrifice. Oh, it brings the tears into our eyes, and the blood into our cheeks, that any should trample on the precious blood, and speak ill of the vicarious sufferings of Christ! Whoever the men may be, yea, though they were angels from heaven, we could not have patience with them. We cannot help regarding those as worse than carrion-crows who would desire to touch this sublimest though simplest of all doctrines, that Jesus Christ bore our sins in his own body on the tree. They dare to say that it is immoral to suppose that our sin could be transferred to Christ, or his righteousness to us. Thus, to charge the essential act of grace with immorality, is to profane the sacrifice of God, and count the blood of Jesus an unholy thing.[52]

---

[52] *MTP*, 33:639–40.

PART 4

THE NEW LIFE

CHAPTER 8

THE HOLY SPIRIT AND SANCTIFICATION

The Life of the Spirit Is Communion with Christ

A strong mark of Spurgeon's theology of the Christian life is his insistence that the Spirit who imparts the first germ of life into sinners will not stop there. The Spirit would not have people "merely saved" from judgment. The author of life is the preserver and increaser of it.[1] That is not because the Spirit has a fondness for some abstract blessing called "life" but because of who he is. He is, said Spurgeon,

> the self-same Spirit which abode without measure in our Lord Jesus Christ. We have a union of experience with Christ in the fact that the same oil which anointed him anoints us, the same dew which fell upon his branch refreshes ours, the same holy fire which burned in his breast is kindled in ours.[2]

It is the Spirit himself, in his own person, who enters into the hearts he renews, and his presence cannot but bring the very life of God. The consuming fire that is God himself comes to dwell in the children of God. For "it is not said, 'I will put the grace of my Spirit, I will put the work of my Spirit,' but, 'I will put *my Spirit* within you.' It is the Holy Ghost himself who in

---

[1] "The Personality of the Holy Ghost," in *NPSP*, 1:28.
[2] *MTP*, 18:225.

very deed lives in . . . every new heart and right spirit."[3] And as the Spirit
of Christ he unites us with Christ, sharing with us Jesus's own experience
of anointing.

Spurgeon's understanding of the Spirit thus reinforced and explained
his own experience. His conversion had been the moment when he first
obeyed the summons to look to Jesus Christ for life. That was a work of
the Spirit, whose task it is to bear witness to Jesus (John 15:26). And from
that moment, that remained Spurgeon's ongoing and daily experience of
the Spirit: being turned to look to Christ. Thus he never saw the Spirit's
work of sanctification as having any other basic agenda. Sanctification is
an essentially Christ-centered matter of turning away from other things to
him who conforms us into his own glory. "And we all, with unveiled face,
beholding the glory of the Lord, are being transformed into the same image
from one degree of glory to another. For this comes from the Lord who is
the Spirit" (2 Cor. 3:18). It meant that his message to one and all, Christian
and non-Christian alike, was "look to Christ."

> I would say to any sinner here, whoever you may be, come, friend, come
> along with me to the cross. One says, "But I cannot go with you; you have
> been a minister of the gospel these thirty years and more." My dear friend,
> I am a poor sinner still; and I have to look to Christ every day as I did at
> the very first. Come along with me. Come along with me. It is many, many
> years since, on a snowy morning, I looked to him, and was lightened. I
> wish that, this snowy night, some soul here would look to him and live.[4]

Growth in the Christian life is not, therefore, something very different
from the initial experience of conversion. It is, first and foremost, about
turning to Christ in faith and love. It is, consequently, about increasing *likeness to Christ*. In Spurgeon's mind and teaching, holiness could never be
separated from Christlikeness. "Oh to be Christly!" he prayed. "We do desire
to live on earth the life of Jesus—sent into the world by Him as He was sent
into the world by the Father. We would closely copy all His acts, words, and
spirit; for so only are we saved, when we are saved from the power of sin,
and transformed into the likeness of Christ."[5]

In 1882, Spurgeon preached a sermon in his beloved Mediterranean

3 *MTP*, 18:224.
4 *MTP*, 39:142.
5 C. H. Spurgeon, *The Pastor in Prayer* (London: Elliot Stock, 1893), 44.

retreat of Mentone, titled "Communion with Christ and His People." In it he explained some of the ways in which the Christian life is communion with Christ. Believers, he explained, enjoy their union with Christ primarily through the direct communion of prayer. Moreover, we have communion with Christ in his thoughts and views. The things that please Jesus begin to please us, and the things that grieve Jesus begin to grieve us.

> Consider, for instance, the greatest theme of our thought, and see whether our thoughts are not like those of Christ. He delights in the Father, he loves to glorify the Father; do not we? Is not the Father the centre of our soul's delight? Do we not rejoice at the very sound of his name? Does not our spirit cry, "Abba, Father"? Thus it is clear that we feel as Jesus feels towards the Father, and so we have the truest communion with him. This is but one instance; your contemplations will bring before you a wide variety of topics, wherein we think with Jesus.[6]

We also have communion with Christ in our emotions as we begin to share his horror at sin and evil, as we begin to weep with him over the lost, and as we grow in our zeal for God. So too in our actions, we share his life in our actions as we pray, as we deny ourselves, as we teach, as we do good to others, and as we seek to make peace. "Wherever, indeed, we co-operate with the Lord Jesus in his designs of love to men, we are in true and active communion with him."[7] And in our sorrows and joys we share Christ's griefs and Christ's reproaches as well as Christ's happiness and Christ's victories.

To say, then, that the Christian life, for Spurgeon, *is* communion with Christ absolutely does not imply that Christians are called to a monastic existence, away from the world. Christians are called to be like Christ, separated from *sin* but not from people. After all, as Spurgeon said elsewhere, "nobody mixed more with sinners than did our Lord."[8] And particularly, if we are to have true communion with Christ, we must, like him, cherish communion with his people. That means that as we share *his* thoughts, emotions, actions, sorrows, and joys, so we must seek to be of one mind with fellow believers and share each other's passions, actions, trials, and joys.

> Let it be our delight to find our society in the circle of which Jesus is the centre, and let us make those our friends who are the friends of Jesus. By

---

[6] "Communion with Christ and His People," in *MTP*, 58:147.
[7] "Communion with Christ and His People," in *MTP*, 58:147.
[8] *MTP*, 27:513.

frequent united prayer and praise, and by ministering the one to the other the things which we have learned by the Spirit, we shall have fellowship with each other in our Lord Jesus Christ.[9]

Sanctification by the Blood of Christ

How exactly does the Spirit turn us to Christ and conform us into his image? What are the means he uses? So much in church life will depend on the answer to this question, and so Spurgeon wanted to be clear: true godliness cannot be fostered in Christians "by mere excitement, by crowded meetings, by the stamping of the foot, or the knocking of the pulpit cushion, or the delirious bawlings of ignorant zeal."[10] Such things can have only superficial effects on lives. There is, in the end, only one answer: the Holy Spirit "must come into the living heart *through living truth*, and so bring nutriment and stimulant to the pining spirit, for so only can it be revived."[11] In other words, it is *as the Spirit of truth* that the Spirit sanctifies (John 16:13; 17:17).

All of God's holy Word has a sanctifying effect, but Spurgeon held that there is a condensed kernel at its center, supremely potent in its ability to create holiness. That is the blood of Christ. The very same blood the Spirit uses to regenerate the dead is the blood that sanctifies the living. To illustrate, Spurgeon once depicted the Christian as a sin-stained garment that needs to be washed. For the garment to be washed there must be (1) a person to wash it and (2) a bath in which it is to be washed: "The person is the Holy Spirit, but the bath is the precious blood of Christ."[12]

The first verse of Augustus Toplady's hymn "Rock of Ages" captured the essence of Spurgeon's thinking here, and he returned to its imagery often:

> Rock of Ages, cleft for me,
> Let me hide myself in Thee;
> Let the water and the blood,
> From Thy riven side which flowed,
> Be of sin the double cure,
> Cleanse me from its guilt and power.

Apart from the Sinai imagery, two biblical texts are here brought together and applied: the fountain of cleansing in Zechariah 13:1, and the flow of

---

[9] "Communion with Christ and His People," in *MTP*, 58:149.
[10] *S&T: 1866*, 98.
[11] *S&T: 1866*, 99, my emphasis.
[12] *MTP*, 8:93.

blood and water from Christ's side when pierced by the soldier's spear in John 19:34. This second scene Spurgeon saw as an emblem of the double cleansing which we find in Jesus.[13] That is, from Christ's blood-work on the cross we receive both pardon and purification, blood atoning and water washing. Flowing together from Christ's side, they are distinct but cannot be disconnected. "The washing which takes away the offence before heaven removes also the love of offending."[14] When Spurgeon came to preach on Zechariah 13:1, he therefore said:

> Blessed be the Lord, when he opened the fountain to cleanse his sinful people, he made it "of sin the double cure," that it might at the same time cleanse us from its guilt and power. For our double need there is, according to the text, one only supply; no mention is made of two fountains, neither are there two methods for the putting away of sin. But the one method is divine, God himself has devised, ordained, and prepared it. Wouldst thou have sin forgiven thee? Wash, for there is a fountain opened. Wouldst thou have sin eradicated from thy nature, and thy heart made pure? Wash, for heaven declares that the fountain is opened for this also.[15]

Just, then, as there can be no life without the cross, there can be no *growth* in the Christian life apart from the cross. "Can you behold him in the depth of shame without pining to lift him up to the heights of glory? Can you see him stooping thus for you without pleading with God that a glorious high throne may be his, and that he may sit upon it and rule all the hearts of men?"[16] At the cross our pride and sinfulness are mortified, our self-deifying efforts are damned, our wandering hearts exposed, and the beauty of Christ in his humility and holiness are held before us. *There* is best displayed the love of Christ, which is "the transfiguring power in the hand of the Holy Spirit."[17] There the glory of God shines brightest in all its transforming power.

The Spirit Makes Lively People

"From my very soul," Spurgeon once wrote, "I detest everything that in the least savours of the Antinomianism which leads people to prate about

---

13 *MTP*, 23:265.
14 *MTP*, 17:39.
15 *MTP*, 17:39.
16 *MTP*, 23:270.
17 *MTP*, 34:335.

being secure in Christ while they are living in sin."[18] That abhorrence of antinomianism was the consequence of everything we have seen so far: the Spirit is the Spirit of *Christ*, the Spirit of *life*, and so *must* make a difference in a person. With the Spirit, there can be no such thing as "a mere foren-sic justification, apart from a spiritual work within the soul,—a change of heart, and a renewal of mind."[19] He has no abstract salvation or blessing to give that could leave a person unchanged. He has the life of Christ to share with us.

The force of Spurgeon's statements here could lead some Protestants to fear that he was muddying the distinction between justification (which is by faith alone) and sanctification. In actual fact he was quite clear: "It is faith that saves us, *not* works, but the faith that saves us always *produces* works."[20] Holiness acquires no merit before God for salvation, but it is, Spurgeon held, the visible manifestation of a heart that has been renewed and knows God's forgiveness.[21] And this, he explained, is just what we see in Hebrews 11, that great paean of faith:

> The eleventh of Hebrews is a chapter dedicated to the glorification of faith; but if I assert that it records the good works of the saints, can any-body contradict me? Is it not as much a record of works as of faith? Ay, verily, because where there is much faith, there shall surely ere long be abundant good works. I have no notion of that faith which does not pro-duce good works, especially in the preacher.[22]

When considering the work of the Spirit in believers, Spurgeon liked to speak of how the Spirit of life makes lively people. As the Son of God is dynamically and fully alive in the Spirit, so he makes the children of God spiritually active and energetic. This is what *life* means. The idea of a pas-sive Christian, content in sin, content not to know God better, was simply anathema to this understanding of the Spirit. No, "wherever the grace of God is, it makes a difference. A graceless man is not like a gracious man; and a gracious man is not like a graceless one."[23]

This spiritual liveliness is primarily an internal thing. Just as Jesus, the Spirit-anointed Christ, was motivated by an internal zeal for God, a

---

[18] *Autobiog.*, 1:258.
[19] *ARM*, 379.
[20] *MTP*, 21:89, my emphasis.
[21] *ARM*, 309.
[22] *ARM*, 21.
[23] *MTP*, 58:589.

love for his Father that manifested itself in obedience (John 4:34; 14:31), so the Spirit gives the children of God new loves. He takes away the love of sin and implants a love for God and his holy ways.[24] Yet that new life cannot *remain* a purely internal thing. "You must be aware that there are some professed followers of Christ whose whole religious life is inward; to tell you the truth, there is no life at all; but their own profession is that it is all inward."[25] The new loves that the Spirit implants will show themselves: hating sin, the Christian will battle it; loving God, the Christian will strive to know him, please him, and walk in his ways.

The active, spiritual life (*zoē*) of the Christian is thus quite different from the passive, merely biological life (*bios*) of plants. "Depend upon it, you and I do not grow holy by going to sleep. People are not made to grow in grace as plants grow, of which it is said, 'They grow ye know not how.'"[26] Rather, the Spirit makes the Christian active. He does not do the work of repenting, believing, and working *for* us; he leads us to do these things willingly *ourselves*. He works in us to act, but the action is our own. "We repent and we believe, and we do good works, because he causes us to do so. A willing walk with God is a sweet result of the Holy Spirit's indwelling."[27]

On the other hand, while it is we who are active, our activity is, importantly, *of the Spirit*. And that was a great personal comfort to Spurgeon, for it meant he was not left to himself. He once described in a sermon how he had recently been in a state of icy spiritual dullness, unmoved by the thought of the cross and God's love, without any warmth of affection toward Christ or the Father:

> My heart sank within me for a moment, but only for a moment, for there flashed across me this thought,—"The Holy Spirit can produce within your heart all those emotions you are seeking for, all those desires you fain would feel, all the meltings, and the movings, and the yearnings, and the rejoicings, which are significant of the grace of God."
>
> Under the influence of that truth, as in a moment, my deadness and coldness were driven away, and I was filled with adoring love. . . . And when, by faith, I perceived that he could not only there and then give me to feel spiritual life, but could maintain it against all hazards, and perfect it beyond all imperfections, and bring me safe into his eternal kingdom

---

[24] *MTP*, 58:590.
[25] *MTP*, 50:460.
[26] *MTP*, 57:173.
[27] *MTP*, 18:226.

and glory; an act of faith exerted upon the Holy Spirit through the cross of
Christ made my soul eager for prayer, and my joy and peace in believing
were more than restored to me![28]

The first part of the Spirit's enlivening is a work to rescue us from
the stultifying and deadening effects of sin. And if it is true that sin is a
wretched slavery, it would be ungracious for the Spirit to leave us in it.

> Many people think that when we preach salvation, we mean salvation
> from going to hell. We do not mean *that*, but we mean a great deal more;
> we preach salvation *from sin*; we say that Christ is able to save a man; and
> we mean by that that he is able to save him from sin and to make him
> holy; to make him a new man. No person has any right to say, "I am saved,"
> while he continues in sin as he did before. How can you be saved from sin
> while you are living in it? A man that is drowning cannot say he is saved
> from the water while he is sinking in it; a man that is frost-bitten cannot
> say, with any truth, that he is saved from the cold while he is stiffened in
> the wintry blast. No, man, Christ did not come to save thee *in* thy sins, but
> to save thee *from* thy sins; not to make the disease so that it should not kill
> thee, but to let it remain in itself mortal, and, nevertheless, to remove it
> from thee, and thee from it.[29]

But again, the Spirit will not drive out sin *for us*. He will lead, empower,
and guide, but it is we who must pick up the sword. "Sin is to be driven
out of us as the Canaanites were driven out of Canaan by the edge of the
sword. . . . Weary may be your march, but march you must if you would
conquer."[30] And Spurgeon was clear that this fight is not only against the
sins and weaknesses of the body, but also against the sins and weaknesses
of the mind. As much as we confront our own impurity, we must confront
our doubt.[31]

The second part of the Spirit's enlivening is positive: as well as being
a spirit of fire and light, consuming our dross and chasing away our dark-

---

[28] *MTP*, 18:217–18.
[29] *MTP*, 11:138.
[30] *MTP*, 57:173.
[31] That said, Spurgeon urged special caution in dealing with such a wily adversary as Satan:

> We cannot convert or convince the devil; it is better to refer him to our Lord. When he tells
> me I am not a saint, I answer, "Well, what am I, then?" "A sinner," says he. "Well, so are you!"
> "Ah!" saith he, "you will be lost." "No," say I, "that is why I shall not be lost, since Jesus Christ
> came into the world to save sinners, and I therefore trust in him to save me." This is what
> Martin Luther calls cutting the devil's head off with his own sword, and it is the best course
> you can follow. (*MTP*, 33:383–84)

ness, he breathes into us his own heavenly nature.[32] This is "the Spirit's work in the soul, by which a man is made like God, and becomes a partaker of the divine nature."[33] It is the life and holy atmosphere of heaven begun now in the saint on earth. "There is no change in the substance of the new life when we enter glory, only it grows and develops and reaches perfection in heaven. The believer's life on earth is Christ; his life in heaven is the same."[34] It is a growing life that gathers and cannot be destroyed, giving believers now the assurance that "this poor heart of ours will yet become perfect as God is perfect; and our nature through his indwelling shall rise into complete meetness for the inheritance of the saints in light."[35]

While the nature that the Spirit gives believers is heavenly, it is not otherworldly. It is for builders, farmers, and homemakers just as much as it is for pastors and preachers. It is a nature that will make homemakers into "sisters of mercy" in their homes, and make "men who are deacons for Christ in common life." For, said Spurgeon, "Christ did not come into the world to take all fishermen from their nets."[36] The Spirit's aim in sanctification is to separate us from sin, not society.

One other important caveat is worth mentioning here. Spurgeon was prepared to speak in strong terms of the transformation the Spirit can work in believers as he makes gracious saints of vicious sinners:

> Our Lord can put so much of himself, by means of his love, into the hearts of his people, that they may be mistaken for himself. John made a blunder in heaven, and fell at the feet of one of his brethren the prophets; for he had come to be so much like his Lord, that John could hardly tell the one from the other. Had he forgotten that word, "We shall be like him; for we shall see him as he is" [1 John 3:2]?[37]

Yet none of the saved on earth are yet perfect. While it is true that believers shall, ultimately, be perfected in the image of Christ, and while we yearn for that perfection now, we shall not enjoy that perfection until the resurrection.[38] "No, no; I cannot believe that the flesh can be perfect, nor, consequently, that a man can be perfect in this flesh. I cannot believe

---

[32] *MTP*, 27:661.
[33] *MTP*, 50:458.
[34] *MTP*, 27:662.
[35] *MTP*, 18:225.
[36] *MTP*, 7:413.
[37] *MTP*, 34:334–35.
[38] *Autobiog.*, 1:258.

that we shall ever live to see people walking up and down in this world without sin."[39] Clarity on this was especially important for Spurgeon as he opposed the Higher Life and Holiness movements, which taught various forms of perfectionism in his day. He was even prepared to be quite fierce in exposing the delusions of those who felt they had attained perfection. In his autobiography he wrote:

> I met in my first pastorate, as I have often done since, a number of persons who professed to be perfect, and who said that they had lived so many months or years without sinning against God. One man, who told me that he was perfect, was hump-backed; and when I remarked that I thought, if he were a perfect man, he ought to have a perfect body, he became so angry that I said to him, "Well, my friend, if *you* are perfect, there are a great many more as near perfection as you are." "Oh!" he exclaimed, "I shall feel it for having been betrayed into anger." He said that he had not been angry for many years; I had brought him back to his old state of infirmity, and painful as it might be for him, I have no doubt that it did him good to see himself as he really was.[40]

A Matter of the Heart

There is simply no other way to put this: for Spurgeon, the heart of sanctification is the sanctification of the heart. The Holy Spirit sanctifies though God's truth, but mere comprehension of new knowledge, however heavenly, is not sanctification. Spurgeon held that heartless orthodoxy is quite as bad as heartless unbelief—in fact, that it is the other side of the same coin. Equally, while the work of sanctification must involve a change of behavior, a mere change of behavior without a change of heart is at best but superficial and at worst rankly hypocritical. True holiness is a deep matter of those desires and loves that then drive our actions.

> Morality does but skim the surface, holiness goes into the very caverns of the great deep; holiness requires that the heart shall be set on God, and that it shall beat with love to him. The moral man may be complete in his morality without that. Methinks I might draw such a parallel as this. Morality is a sweet, fair corpse, well washed and robed, and even embalmed with spices; but holiness is the living man,

39 *MTP*, 57:176–77.
40 *Autobiog.*, 1:261–62.

as fair and as lovely as the other, but having life. Morality lies there, of the earth, earthy, soon to be food for corruption and worms; holiness waits and pants with heavenly aspirations, prepared to mount and dwell in immortality beyond the stars. These twain are of opposite nature; the one belongs to this world, the other belongs to that world beyond the skies. It is not said in heaven, "Moral, moral, moral art thou, O God!" but "Holy, holy, holy art thou, O Lord!" You note the difference between the two words at once. The one, how icy cold; the other, oh, how animated![41]

That being the case, sanctification cannot be a mechanical process. It is a matter of the Spirit wooing and turning hearts so that believers might not just *act* differently but *think* differently and *want* differently and *therefore* act differently.

The statutes of the Lord are the delight of his saints. There are sweet inducements which the Holy Spirit applies to them, whereby their heart is inclined to keep God's commandments. We are not to look upon Gospel holiness as being a forced fruit from any man. Holiness is essentially voluntary. The Spirit of God educates while he operates upon the mind; hence, when the understanding is enlightened to see the beauty of holiness, the will is certain to seek after it.[42]

A Growing Delight

In order to make us holy, the Spirit animates us to a particular sort of love above all: that love *which finds its joy in God*. Spurgeon wrote and preached a good deal on joy. Read, for example, "Bells for the Horses" (on Zech. 14:20),[43] "Joy Born at Bethlehem" (on Luke 2:10–12),[44] "The Joy of the Lord, the Strength of His People" (on Neh. 8:10),[45] "Joy, a Duty" (on Phil. 4:4),[46] "Joy in God" (on Rom. 5:11),[47] "How to Become Full of Joy" (on 1 John 1:4).[48] In fact, Spurgeon was eager to emphasize the vital importance of joy precisely because of how maligned and marginalized he felt joy to be in his day.

---

[41] *MTP*, 50:459–60.
[42] Charles H. Spurgeon, *C. H. Spurgeon's Sermons beyond Volume 63: An Authentic Supplement to the Metropolitan Tabernacle Pulpit: Forty-Five Forgotten Sermons Compiled from the Baptist Messenger* (Leominster: Day One, 2009), 493.
[43] *S&T: 1866*, 33–40.
[44] "Joy Born at Bethlehem," in *MTP*, 17:697–708.
[45] "The Joy of the Lord, the Strength of His People," in *MTP*, 17:709–20.
[46] "Joy, a Duty," in *MTP*, 41:133–42.
[47] "Joy in God," in *MTP*, 44:1–9.
[48] "How to Become Full of Joy," in *MTP*, 57:493–501.

Some people are so afraid of joy, that one might suppose them to labour under the delusion that all who are devout must also be unhappy. If we worshipped Baal, to lance ourselves with knives were most fitting, if we were worshippers of Juggernaut or Kalee, self-inflicted tortures might be acceptable; if we adored the pope, it might be proper for us to wear a hair shirt and practise flagellation; but as we worship the ever-blessed God, whose delight is to make his creatures happy, holy happiness is a part of worship, and joy in the Lord one of the accepted graces of the Holy Spirit. Brethren, let us be happy when we praise God. I have noticed with pain the way in which people will get rid, if they can, of happy words out of their hymns. The hundredth Psalm for instance, runs thus:—

> "All people that on earth do dwell,
> Sing to the Lord with cheerful voice,
> Him serve with——"

What? Well, they modernise it into—

> "Him serve with *fear*."

But, as I believe, the older form is—

> "Him serve with *mirth*, his praise forth tell,
> Come ye before him and rejoice."

I wonder some other scribe did not cut out the word "cheerful," and put in—

> "Sing to the Lord with *doleful* voice."

In this way the Psalm might have been "improved" until there would not have been a grain of worship left in it. I mean to sing it, "Him serve with *mirth*;" and with a glad and merry heart will I praise my God.[49]

Yet Spurgeon's championing of joy was not a mere reaction to the religious Eeyores of his day; it flowed directly from his understanding of the gospel. "What is the gospel?" he once asked. "Glad tidings of great joy."[50] And why? For the gospel reveals a happy God. The happiness of God was a

---

[49] *MTP*, 16:70.
[50] "Joy, a Duty," in *MTP*, 41:136.

theme Spurgeon returned to again and again. He held that it "enters into the essential idea of God that he is superlatively blessed. We cannot conceive of a God who should be infinitely miserable."[51] Being infinitely full of happiness, God is a God who delights to share his happiness, and who created us for that very reason. "He is the happy God; ineffable bliss is the atmosphere in which he lives, and he would have his people to be happy . . . for a joyous God desires a joyous people."[52]

Our problem as humans is that, having been made to find happiness in God, we instinctively (and vainly) look for it elsewhere. "Since man fell in the garden, he has too often sought for his enjoyments where the serpent finds his."[53] Yet the richest gladness is found only in communion with the happy God.

> If I were asked what is the sweetest frame within the whole compass of human feeling, I should not speak of a sense of power in prayer, or abundant revelation, or rapturous joys, or conquest of evil spirits; but I should mention, as the most exquisite delight of my being, a condition of conscious dependence upon God.[54]

The Christian life, then, is one of entering into what Spurgeon called "the noblest and truest immortality," whereby we "live as God liveth, in peace and joy, and happiness."[55] By rejoicing in the Lord, we "commence our heaven here below."[56] Christians rejoice in the Lord always. We rejoice in the privileges and blessings of the gospel, and will know a special joy when we walk in holiness and close communion with Christ.[57] Above all, though—above all the blessings of salvation and adoption—it is God in himself who is the great object of our joy. Thus when our hearts or circumstances leave us feeling that we cannot rejoice in anything else, we can still rejoice, for we rejoice in One who is unchangeably joy-giving.[58] "He is everything to us—our joy, our hope, our all. Our bliss depends, not upon what we are in ourselves, but upon what he is in himself."[59]

It all makes for a Christian experience that is very surprising to the

---

51 *S&T: 1866*, 35.
52 "Joy, a Duty," in *MTP*, 41:136.
53 "The Joy of the Lord, the Strength of His People," in *MTP*, 17:710.
54 *ARM*, 182.
55 *MTP*, 17:384.
56 "Joy, a Duty," in *MTP*, 41:134.
57 *ARM*, 363.
58 "Joy, a Duty," in *MTP*, 41:137–38.
59 *S&T: 1882*, 140.

outsider. The non-Christian assumes that religion means only service and duty, never pleasure or delight. Religion is the grim price to pay for earning heaven or escaping hell. Yet, when looking at Psalm 37:4 ("Delight yourself in the LORD"), Spurgeon noted:

> The life of the believer is here described as a *delight* in God, and we are thus certified of the great fact that true religion overflows with happiness and joy. . . . We fear not God because of any compulsion; our faith is no fetter, our profession is no bondage, we are not dragged to holiness, nor driven to duty. No, our piety is our pleasure, our hope is our happiness, our duty is our delight.[60]

In Christ the believer finds a God whose yoke is easy and whose burden is light (Matt. 11:30).[61] Instead of serving him in sour resignation, we find we actually bring *ourselves* pleasure when we walk in his ways. "Man cannot please God without bringing to himself a great amount of happiness."[62] Moreover, true Christlikeness involves desiring to enjoy God ever more.[63] And when we do so, we find we *must* rejoice, for true joy in the Lord "must speak; it cannot hold its tongue, it must praise the name of the Lord."[64]

All of this might have been surprising to many who heard Spurgeon, but he was emphatic that his thoroughgoing emphasis on joy was no personal whimsy born of a jovial disposition. It was part and parcel of his theological inheritance from the Puritans:

> The Puritans were never accused of too much hilarity, but they were, as a rule, happy men; and one of them shall speak from the grave in support of the duty which I am now urging upon you. Ho, Master Thomas Watson, let us hear thy voice from thy sepulchre! These are the words which my ear drinks in from him who discoursed so sweetly upon "Divine Contentment:" "Cheerfulness honours religion; it proclaims to the world that we serve a good Master; cheerfulness is a friend to grace; it puts the heart in tune to serve God. Uncheerful Christians, like the spies, bring an evil report on the good land; others suspect there is something unpleasant in religion, that they who profess it hang their harps upon the willows, and walk so dejectedly. Be serious, yet cheerful. Rejoice in the

---

60 Charles H. Spurgeon, *Morning and Evening: Daily Readings*, complete and unabridged, new modern ed. (Peabody, MA: Hendrickson, 2006), morning, June 14.
61 *MTP*, 18:226–27.
62 *NPSP*, 3:1.
63 *MTP*, 16:66.
64 "Joy, a Duty," in *MTP*, 41:135.

Lord alway." Well said, Master Watson, may we all have grace to practise thy good counsel![65]

As Spurgeon saw it, joy in God is part of the very fiber of Christian vitality, and thus he would connect it to every other aspect of holiness. This could be quite striking, as when he connected the enjoyment of God with both *jealousy* and *fear*. Joy in God, he believed, makes us jealous for Christ, so giving us a stern intolerance of all the sin that grieves him. When the Lord makes a believer

> to be joyed and overjoyed with the sweet consciousness that he is the Beloved's, and that the Beloved is his, then a holy jealousy burns within the soul, and the heart cries, "Is there anything that can grieve the Beloved? Let it be slain! Is there aught that I think, or wish, or say, or do, that might break the sacred spell of communion, and cause him to be gone? Let it be driven out at once!"[66]

Joy in God is also instrumental in that most sacred motive, the fear of the Lord. A true enjoyment and appreciation of God as holy, exalted, and almighty produces a right fear of him. This is not the sort of fear a criminal would have before a judge, or a child would have before a monster; it is "the fear which bows the tall archangel *in adoration* before the throne, the fear which makes the cherub veil his face with his wings *while he adores* the Lord. Such a constant fear as this is the mainspring of Christian holiness."[67]

Since we are made to be happy in Christ, joy is an essential part of human health. When a person is full of joy, "it shines out of his eyes, it sparkles in his countenance . . . it quickens the flowing of the blood in the veins; it is a healthy thing in all respects."[68] Joy has many clear health-giving properties, Spurgeon argued in various places. It is, in that sense, the handmaiden of holiness. Joy in the Lord has the power to strengthen believers against temptation, for when we find our happiness and satisfaction in him, we will not seek it elsewhere.[69] Joy has a medicinal power to cure the ills that come from grumbling. It therefore has the ability to drive

---

[65] *S&T: 1866*, 34.
[66] *MTP*, 27:3.
[67] *MTP*, 57:178, my emphasis.
[68] "Joy, a Duty," in *MTP*, 41:134.
[69] "The Joy of the Lord, the Strength of His People," in *MTP*, 17:715.

away quarreling and promote peace. It is the cure for fretfulness and anxi-ety.[70] And it is a contagious good, as cheer in one quickens cheerfulness in others, so spreading its own benefits.[71]

For these reasons, Spurgeon wrote that with every year in ministry he grew more confident that "the joy of the Lord is and must be our strength, and that discontent and moroseness are fatal to usefulness."[72] This joy is, in fact, "the sign and symbol of strong spiritual life. Holy vivacity betokens spiritual vigour."[73] And that, quite simply, is because it is impossible to enjoy close communion with the happy God without being affected. God's presence is gloriously transformative: his presence must strengthen the weak, purify the corrupt, and cheer the gloomy so that they become like him. "A man who walks in the sunlight of God's countenance, for that very reason is warm and strong. The sunlight of joy usually goes with the warmth of spiritual life."[74]

Christians must, then, *fight* for joy, and *fight* for that intimacy with God that fosters joy. We will see in chapter 11 that, perhaps surprisingly, Spurgeon's own personal inclination was toward a state of melancholy. But, he averred, if

> we once begin to give way to this foolishness, we shall soon forge chains for ourselves that we cannot easily break. Take down your harp from the willow, believer. Do not let your fingers neglect the well-known strings. Come, let us be happy and joyful! If we have looked sad for a while, let us now be brightened by thoughts of Christ.[75]

Despondency, he knew from personal experience, has a leeching effect on us. It saps vitality, replacing praise and thanksgiving with a grumble. Therefore, Spurgeon advised, "to maintain an inward spring of thanksgiv-ing is one of the best ways to keep yourselves in spiritual health."[76] But it is not just a *lack* of joy that threatens the Christian; a *misplaced* joy is equally dangerous. So "take care that you *rejoice in the Lord when you have other things to rejoice in*. When he loads your table with good things, and your cup is overflowing with blessings, rejoice in *him* more than in *them*."[77]

---

[70] "Joy, a Duty," in *MTP*, 41:133–34.
[71] "Joy, a Duty," in *MTP*, 41:135.
[72] *S&T: 1866*, 34.
[73] "The Joy of the Lord, the Strength of His People," in *MTP*, 17:715.
[74] "The Joy of the Lord, the Strength of His People," in *MTP*, 17:715.
[75] "How to Become Full of Joy," in *MTP*, 57:495.
[76] *MTP*, 16:71.
[77] "Joy, a Duty," in *MTP*, 41:138.

A Growing Disgust

That growing pleasure in God that the Christian enjoys has a necessary flip side, Spurgeon taught: the more desire we have for God and his righteousness, the more disgust we will have at sin. "He who sincerely repents of sin will hate it, and find no pleasure in it, and during the season when his heart is broken, he will loathe even to detestation the very approach of evil."[78] And this, too, is a growing disposition. On conversion, a young Christian may feel he is a wretched sinner, but his knowledge of his own sinfulness will actually be very superficial. The Spirit's enlightening work over the years that follow is thus quite bittersweet, for enlightening means not only knowing God better but also knowing self better. The Spirit enables us to see ever deeper into our own darkness, the depths of which would simply overwhelm the young believer. Mature Christians therefore *feel* themselves to be greater sinners than do young Christians. It is not that they are; rather, the Spirit has made them more *sensitive* to sin and more averse to it. Those sins we once ignored as petty and worth no attention become to us a source of ever-deeper pain.[79]

Yet, at the same time, the Spirit works to educate the Christian in the gospel, the power of Christ's blood, and the nature of holiness. Thus, while the Christian's own sense of personal sin grows, it is no longer mixed with a fear of hell. Where once we might have fled sin out of fear of punishment, increasingly we flee it out of fear of itself. Sin *itself* begins to horrify and disgust us.

> The nearer you get to perfection, the more horrified you feel because of the sin that still remains in you; and the more horror you feel at your sin, the more intense will be your gratitude to the bleeding Saviour who has put that sin away; and, in consequence, the more intense will be your love to him.[80]

None of this means that growth in holiness means growth in sadness. Sorrow for sin, Spurgeon felt, is a "sweet sorrow," because as we repent, we feel our Father's pleasure and we share it. While the battle is hard, and the presence of sin in us is offensive to us, we *enjoy* opposing the darkness. Spurgeon once confessed, "I do not know, beloved, when I am more

---

[78] *NPSP*, 1:406.
[79] *MTP*, 57:172.
[80] *MTP*, 50:114.

perfectly happy than when I am weeping for sin at the foot of the cross."[81]
We also enjoy repentance for how it always leads to deeper joy. Confessing
our sin throws us afresh onto the grace of Jesus and leads us to the cross;
opposing sin makes us stand closer to him.

> So, when the soul has been saturated with the rain of penitence, the
> clear shining of forgiving love makes the flowers of gladness blossom all
> around. The steps by which we ascend to the palace of delight are usually
> moist with tears. Grief for sin is the porch of the House Beautiful, where
> the guests are full of "The joy of the Lord."[82]

Sorrow for sin flows from the distaste experienced by those who are waking
up to the superior and opposite pleasures of holiness and life in Christ. It is
a reaction to the hellish by those who belong in heaven.

---

81 "How to Become Full of Joy," in *MTP*, 57:497.
82 "The Joy of the Lord, the Strength of His People," in *MTP*, 17:710.

CHAPTER 9

PRAYER

One expects theologians and pastors to say that prayer is important. Talk is cheap. Yet Spurgeon's high regard for prayer would prove itself in his life and ministry. He would often get especially passionate when pleading with his people to pray: "Oh, for God's sake, for his name and glory's sake, if you would honour the Father, if you would let Jesus see of the travail of his soul, wrestle together with us in your prayers for the divine working."[1] Every week, it was the Monday night main prayer meeting that underpinned the life of the church, and normally over a thousand would attend. At church meetings, and especially on Sundays, Spurgeon was remarkably cautious in whom he allowed to lead in public prayer. For, he said, "it is my solemn conviction that the prayer is one of the most weighty, useful, and honourable parts of the service, and that it ought to be even more considered than the sermon. There must be no putting up of anybodies and nobodies to pray, and then the selection of the abler man to preach."[2] Indeed, he went on, "if I may have my choice, I will sooner yield up the sermon than the prayer."[3]

The Breath of Heavenly Life

Spurgeon prized prayer so because he did not view it merely as one Christian activity among others. Prayer is communion with God, which is the

---

[1] "Pleading for Prayer," in *MTP*, 32:120.
[2] *Lectures*, 1:59.
[3] *Lectures*, 1:60.

very nature of eternal life. It is faith in action. It is a taste on earth of the everlasting life of praise Christians will enjoy before the throne of heaven. As such, prayer is an activity the *un*believer will never truly enter into. It is, then, a sure token of regeneration and adoption, evidence that a heart has been reconciled to God and turned to feel dependence on God, love for God, and peace with God. Prayer is the breathing that evidences the new life in Christ. "The habit of private prayer, and the constant practice of heart-fellowship with the Most High, are the surest indicators of the work of the Holy Spirit upon the heart."[4]

None of that is to suggest that Christians, upon conversion, enter into an unsullied life of pure faith and enjoyment of God. Far from it; they remain sinners with a bent away from God and therefore prayer. Yet, Spurgeon said:

> Prayer comes spontaneously from those who abide in Jesus, even as certain oriental trees, without pressure, shed their fragrant gums. Prayer is the natural outgushing of a soul in communion with Jesus. Just as the leaf and the fruit will come out of the vine-branch without any conscious effort on the part of the branch, but simply because of its living union with the stem, so prayer buds, and blossoms, and fruits out of souls abiding in Jesus. As stars shine, so do abiders pray. It is their use and their second nature.[5]

Prayer is the breath of heavenly life: where that life is, there must be some prayer; where that life flourishes, there will be *much* prayer, and much *pleasure* in prayer. "As the man loves God more, and becomes more like Christ, he takes greater delight in prayer."[6]

The life that the Spirit breathes into believers is not one of mere individualistic vertical love for God. Preaching on the Lord's Supper, Spurgeon once exclaimed:

> Brethren, I cannot do without you. If I want to celebrate the Lord's death, I cannot go into my chamber, and take the piece of bread and the cup, and celebrate the ordinance alone; I must have you with me, I cannot do without you. And you, the most spiritually-minded of you, if you shut yourselves up in a cell, and try to play the monk and the super-excellent,

---

4 "'Behold, He Prayeth,'" in *MTP*, 31:505.
5 *MTP*, 34:14–15.
6 *MTP*, 34:634.

cannot keep this ordinance. You must have fellowship with other believers, you must come down among the saints, for our Saviour has given us this memorial which cannot be celebrated except jointly, by the whole of us together.[7]

All who are brought to love Christ begin to love his bride and people as well. True believers will love other believers—and will therefore pray for them. In fact, taught Spurgeon, "you do not love the brethren unless you pray for them, and then [if you do not] it follows you are dead in trespasses and sins."[8] Prayers for the saints flow from influence of the Spirit and serve as "grand cement" for church unity.[9] Where they are lacking, there cannot be spiritual health, and there will soon be division and disunion.

Prayer is, as John Calvin would put it, "the chief exercise of faith."[10] In Spurgeon's words, "He who prays trusts, and thus reveals the faith which saves."[11] Prayer, as he saw it, is the battleground on which faith wars with natural unbelief. In prayer we recognize our own finite creatureliness and sinful unworthiness—and if we don't, we are not truly praying, but sinning. "If you pray as a deserving person, pleading your own good deeds, there is such a lie at the bottom of your prayers that you have not prayed at all."[12] In prayer we also recognize God's infinite ability, graciousness, and worth. Where sin depends on self, doubts God, and distrusts his promises, prayer seeks to prove God's ability and grace by asking. And God loves to be proved in this way, explained Spurgeon. Therefore, "the more you expect from God, the more you are likely to receive. Look for great things from him, and come to him with large requests."[13]

Prayer, then, is not primarily a matter of words, spoken and arranged nicely by those with that ability. Our prayers "are not powerful in proportion to their expression; for, if so, the Pharisee would have succeeded, since he evidently had greater gifts than the Publican had."[14] Rather, prayer is the outpouring of a faithful heart seeking communion with God. That sometimes means a groaning before God too deep for words (Rom. 8:26), and Spurgeon was happy to speak of his own experience of this, and how prayer

---

[7] "The Lord's Supper, Simple but Sublime!," in *MTP*, 55:315–16.
[8] "Intercessory Prayer," in *MTP*, 7:456.
[9] *S&T: 1881*, 171.
[10] John Calvin, *Institutes of the Christian Religion*, ed. John T. McNeill, trans. Ford Lewis Battles (Louisville: Westminster John Knox, 2011), 3.20 (p. 850).
[11] "'Behold, He Prayeth,'" in *MTP*, 31:505.
[12] "'Behold, He Prayeth,'" in *MTP*, 31:511.
[13] "Encouragements to Prayer," in *MTP*, 40:460.
[14] "Comfort for Those Whose Prayers Are Feeble," in *MTP*, 54:126.

for him went beyond his own words. "I like sometimes, in prayer, when I do not feel that I can say anything, just to sit still, and look up. . . . Thus we have intercourse with Jesus of a closer sort than any words could possibly express. . . . I assert that the devout soul can converse with the Lord Jesus all the day."[15]

To be clear, while true prayer is not the mere utterance of words, nor is it the mere feeling of desires. More than either, "it is the advance of the desires to God, the spiritual approach of our nature towards the Lord our God."[16] It is the approach of the believer by the Spirit of God to the throne of God. Yet, because prayer is not a vocal performance, it cannot be a privilege reserved for the articulate; it is the birthright of every child of God. "We cannot all argue, but we can all pray; we cannot all be leaders, but we can all be pleaders; we cannot all be mighty in rhetoric, but we can all be prevalent in prayer. I would sooner see you eloquent with God than with men."[17]

All that being the case, prayer must not only be the living breath of the new life: it must also be the breath of any faithful ministry. Because of what prayer is, no amount of talent or education—wonderful gifts though they may be to the church—can substitute for it. "All our libraries and studies are mere emptiness compared with our closets. We grow, we wax mighty, we prevail in private prayer."[18] Talents and education are good, but they do not in and of themselves contain the spiritual life that prayer has. And this is why Spurgeon was so cautious in whom he allowed to lead in public prayer. His concern was not primarily that they might not be *articulate* but that they might not be sufficiently *holy*. An able but spiritually emaciated man will betray his state in his prayers more quickly than in his preaching. And if he is strong in talent but weak in prayer, over time his congregation will be nurtured in the lie that style matters more than spiritual substance.

> If your zeal grows dull, you will not pray well in the pulpit; you will pray worse in the family, and worst in the study alone. When your soul becomes lean, your hearers, without knowing how or why, will find that your prayers in public have little savour for them; they will feel your barrenness, perhaps, before you perceive it yourself. Your discourses will next betray your declension. You may utter as well-chosen words,

---

15 "Communion with Christ and His People," in *MTP*, 58:146.
16 *MTP*, 17:673.
17 *ARM*, 314.
18 *Lectures*, 1:41.

and as fitly-ordered sentences, as aforetime; but there will be a perceptible loss of spiritual force.[19]

A Matter of the Heart

Given his understanding that prayer is the breath of the new life, Spurgeon was notably strident in emphasizing prayer as a matter of the heart. God's work in regeneration is to turn and renew the heart, and before anything else, prayer is the outpouring of that renewed heart. Therefore, "the state of the heart is of prime importance. The heart is the source, the seat, and the essence of supplication. Prayer with the heart is the heart of prayer: the cry of our soul is the soul of our cry."[20]

In private prayer, that means that the posture of the soul is more important than the posture of the body, the spirit more important than the habit, the affections more important than the expressions—not that those other things are *un*important, but that posture, habit, and expressions can be perfectly well mastered by the hypocrite. And that should liberate Christians to *more* prayer, knowing that prayer is not something to be confined to those precious private times in the prayer closet. Speaking to students who would soon be busy ministers, Spurgeon said:

> As a rule, we ministers ought never to be many minutes without actually lifting up our hearts in prayer. Some of us could honestly say that we are seldom a quarter of an hour without speaking to God, and that not as a duty but as an instinct, a habit of the new nature for which we claim no more credit than a babe does for crying after its mother.[21]

That prayer is a matter of the heart also makes public prayer *what it should be*. When public prayer is earnest and not a show, that will cover over a multitude of grammatical errors and draw others to true communion with God. On the other hand, heartless, lackadaisical public prayer will simply encourage sleepiness for body and soul alike. "Cast your whole soul into the exercise," Spurgeon advised. "If ever your whole manhood was engaged in anything, let it be in drawing near unto God in public."[22]

An image Spurgeon frequently returned to when teaching on prayer

---

[19] *Lectures*, 1:9–10.
[20] *MTP*, 30:536.
[21] *Lectures*, 2:33.
[22] *Lectures*, 1:61.

was that of prayer as incense—the sweet smell rising before the Lord (Ps. 141:2; Rev. 5:8). For the fragrance to rise from the golden bowl of incense, there must be an inner fire to ignite it. There must, in other words, be some heartfelt warmth of sincerity in a prayer for God to receive it.[23] At this point we should be clear: Spurgeon often called for warmth in prayer, but it was always the warmth *of sincerity* he pleaded for.

> As you would avoid a viper, *keep from all attempts to work up spurious fervour in public devotion*. Do not labour to seem earnest. Pray as your heart dictates, under the leading of the Spirit of God, and if you are dull and heavy tell the Lord so. It will be no ill thing to confess your deadness, and bewail it, and cry for quickening; it will be real and acceptable prayer; but simulated ardour is a shameful form of lying. Never imitate those who are earnest. You know a good man who groans, and another whose voice grows shrill when he is carried away with zeal, but do not therefore moan or squeak in order to appear as zealous as they are. Just be natural the whole way through, and ask of God to be guided in it all.[24]

Given his insistence on the heartfelt nature of true prayer, Spurgeon displayed what looked like an allergic reaction to the idea of set prayers and liturgy. Unscripted, extempore prayer is, he believed, the "*most scriptural, and should be the most excellent form of public supplication.*"[25] Liturgy was only invented, he believed, because public prayer is often so poor. But then scripted prayer can be equally poor, and Spurgeon had some bad experiences of that.

> I have been at funerals when the burial service of the church of England has been galloped through so indecorously that it has taken all the grace I had to prevent my throwing a hassock at the creature's head. I have felt so indignant that I have not known what to do, to hear, in the presence of mourners whose hearts were bleeding, a man rattling through the service as if he were paid by the piece, and had more work to follow, and therefore desired to get it through as quickly as possible.[26]

Therefore, he advised, Christians should not prepare their prayers in advance but speak as the soul overflows in the occasion. In practice this

---

[23] See, for example, "Golden Vials Full of Odours," in *MTP*, 18:277–88. Also *Lectures*, 1:44.
[24] *Lectures*, 1:70.
[25] *Lectures*, 1:54.
[26] *Lectures*, 1:60–61.

might mean stumbling over words, broken and poor phrasing, and worse. But spoken from the heart, these are the very best prayers that God ever hears. "The overflowing of the soul is the best praying in the world."[27] God, after all, looks on the heart, and only a prayer from the heart will touch his. And the danger of a heartless, scripted prayer is not simply that we might waste our breath. Worse, "in all likelihood you have daubed your conscience over with the notion that you have prayed, and so you have even done yourself serious harm by a flattering deceit."[28]

"Our Father in Heaven"

To speak of prayer as "communion with God" and leave it there would not be sufficient for Spurgeon. When it came to the topic of prayer, he usually became especially explicit in his Trinitarianism. The Trinity provided the logic and shape of his prayer life. Indeed, he taught, Christians are comforted to pray precisely because God is Father, Son, and Spirit. The Spirit is the one who enables us to present our prayers, and that gives us great assurance that we will be heard, for "*the feeblest prayer, if it be sincere, is written by the Holy Spirit upon the heart, and God will always own the handwriting of the Holy Spirit.*"[29] Moreover, the God to whom the Spirit directs our prayers is our Father, and he has "*a quick ear to hear the breathing of any of his children.*"[30] And we approach him united to his perfect Son, who serves as our Mediator, and "*the Lord Jesus Christ is always ready to take the most imperfect prayer, and perfect it for us.*"[31] Every prayer, then, is a Spirit-led approach to our Father made in dependence upon the Son and his blood shed for us. Considering the Father, Son, and Spirit—and what they do for us in prayer—is the very oxygen of prayer. Thus, it was Trinitarian, Christ-centered advice that Spurgeon would give Christians learning to pray. For example:

> You cannot flourish as a Christian unless you constantly draw near to God in supplication, but your supplications must always be presented through the name of Jesus Christ. His name gives prevalence to prayer; it is not so much your earnestness or sincerity, as his precious blood, that speaks in the ears of God and intercedes for you. Pray ever then with your eye upon

---

27 *MTP*, 34:626.
28 *MTP*, 34:631.
29 "Comfort for Those Whose Prayers Are Feeble," in *MTP*, 54:128.
30 "Comfort for Those Whose Prayers Are Feeble," in *MTP*, 54:128.
31 "Comfort for Those Whose Prayers Are Feeble," in *MTP*, 54:129.

the finished propitiation and the living Intercessor; ever plead the merit of Immanuel, and heaven's gate shall open to you.[32]

It is possible to look through Spurgeon's transcribed prayers and see that he was willing on occasion to address the Spirit and that it was not unusual for him to call directly on Christ, but it was normal for him to address the Father in prayer.[33] The normative shape of Christian, Trinitarian prayer is this: the Father is the one "*to* whom we pray," the Son is the one "*through* whom we pray," and the Holy Spirit is the one "*by* whom we pray."[34]

None of this was theological posturing. Once again, Spurgeon was showing that prayer is an act of entering into an enjoyment of the life for which we have been saved. The Christian life is one of being brought together in Christ to be the Spirit-filled children of God, that we might know the omnipotent Creator as our loving and caring Father. This was a privilege Spurgeon would seize with passion in prayer, and which served him with sturdy comfort in his struggles.

> I have found it a blessed thing, in my own experience, to plead before God that I am His child. When, some months ago, I was racked with pain to an extreme degree, so that I could no longer bear it without crying out, I asked all to go from the room, and leave me alone; and then I had nothing I could say to God but this, "Thou art my Father, and I am Thy child; and Thou, as a Father, art tender and full of mercy. I could not bear to see my child suffer as Thou makest me suffer; and if I saw him tormented as I am now, I would do what I could to help him, and put my arms under him to sustain him. Wilt Thou hide Thy face from me, my Father? Wilt Thou still lay on me Thy heavy hand, and not give me a smile from Thy countenance?" I talked to the Lord as Luther would have done, and pleaded His Fatherhood in real earnest. "Like as a father pitieth his children, so the Lord pitieth them that fear Him." If He a Father let Him show Himself a Father,—so I pleaded; and I ventured to say when they came back who watched me, "I shall never have such agony again from this moment, for God has heard my prayer." I bless God that ease came, and the racking pain never returned. Faith mastered it by laying hold upon God in His own revealed character,—that character in which, in our darkest hour, we are best able to appreciate Him. I think this is why

---

32 *MTP*, 16:62–63.
33 Cf. "Secret Prayer Is the Rest of Christian." "The Pure language," in "Notebooks with Sermon Outlines, Vols 2, 4–9," Spurgeon's College, Heritage Room, (U1) vol. 4, sermon 221, Zeph. 3:9.
34 "Hindrances to Prayer," in *MTP*, 20:512.

that prayer, "*Our Father* which art in Heaven," is given to us, because, when we are lowest, we can still say, "Our Father," and when it is very dark, and we are very weak, our childlike appeal can go up, "Father, help me! Father, rescue me!"[35]

In prayer's enjoyment of our adoption by God, Spurgeon saw two things that need to be held together. The first line of the Lord's Prayer captures them both: (1) "Our Father," (2) "in heaven." To come before God as *our Father* means that we can pray with boldness, assurance, and even joyful familiarity. It means we are not approaching a stranger or an enemy.[36] God has reconciled us to himself, and he would have us enjoy that reconciliation fully. And yet we must remember that he is a Father who sits in awesome holiness on his throne of power *in heaven*. Our boldness and familiarity should never be confused with irreverence or impertinence. Our Father is not our equal, and so while we should come to him with real boldness and joyfulness, we must come with *reverent* boldness and *devout* joyfulness. Thus we say to him "*Hallowed* be your name; your *kingdom* come," for "our Father is still to be regarded as a King, and in prayer we come, not only to our Father's feet, but we come also to the throne of the Great Monarch of the universe. The mercy-seat is a throne, and we must not forget this."[37] It means in prayer that we must remember:

> Thou art on earth, and God is in heaven; multiply not thy words as though thou wert talking to thine equal. Do not speak to God as though thou couldst order him about, and have thy will of him, and he were to be a lackey to thee. Bow low before the Most High; own thyself unworthy to approach him, speaking in the tone of one who is pleading for that which must be a gift of great charity. So shalt thou draw near to God aright; but while thou art humble, have desire in thine eyes, and expectation in thy countenance.[38]

Blood, Sweat, and Glory

Prayer, Spurgeon believed, is the "true gauge" of spiritual health.[39] As a man's voice gets weaker when he is sicker, and as he can be unable even

35 *Autobiog.*, 3:247–48. See also C. H. Spurgeon, *The Letters of Charles Haddon Spurgeon* (London: Marshall Brothers, 1923), 30–31.
36 "Achsah's Asking, a Pattern of Prayer," in *MTP*, 39:279.
37 *MTP*, 17:674.
38 "Achsah's Asking, a Pattern of Prayer," in *MTP*, 39:280.
39 "Hindrances to Prayer," in *MTP*, 20:507.

to call out when seriously unwell, so prayer will decline with spiritual ill-health. When Christians feel they can rely on themselves or find more pleasure in things other than God, prayer will become weak or peter out completely. Yet, in stating such things to his people, Spurgeon did not set himself apart. Every Christian is a sinner, and therefore every Christian is a failure in prayer.

> If any man here should venture to say that he prays as much as he ought, as a student, I should gravely question his statement; and if there be a minister, deacon, or elder present who can say that he believes he is occupied with God in prayer to the full extent to which he might be, I should be pleased to know him. I can only say, that if he can claim this excellence, he leaves me far behind, for I can make no such claim: I wish I could; and I make the confession with no small degree of shame-facedness and confusion, but I am obliged to make it.[40]

Yet, as Spurgeon sought to encourage Christians in prayer, he knew that it is precisely this weakness that so often disheartens them. Many, he said, "are dispirited because they cannot yet pray as advanced believers do."[41] We know our weakness and our failures. We know we should be praying far more frequently and far more heartily. And therefore, we feel, prayer is for other (better) believers, and not really for us. But this is like refusing to take medicine because we feel too ill. It is when we do not feel fit to pray that we most need it. In such times we must pray for prayer—or, as Spurgeon liked to put it, "pray till we pray."[42] And in those times when we do not feel fit for prayer, we must strike quickly, for that is the Devil's hour.

> Now the tempter will whisper, "Do not pray just now; your heart is not in a fit condition for it." My dear brother, you will not become fit for prayer by keeping away from the mercy-seat, but to lie groaning or breathing at its foot is the best preparation for pleading before the Lord. We are not to aim at a self-wrought preparation of our hearts that we may come to God aright, but "the preparations of the heart in man, and the answer of the tongue, are from the Lord." If I feel myself disinclined to pray, then is the time when I need to pray more than ever.[43]

---

40 *Lectures*, 1:47.
41 "Comfort for Those Whose Prayers Are Feeble," in *MTP*, 54:121.
42 "Comfort for Those Whose Prayers Are Feeble," in *MTP*, 54:122–23.
43 "Comfort for Those Whose Prayers Are Feeble," in *MTP*, 54:123.

Turning to prayer when prayer is hard needn't mean going from silence to composing perfect speeches to God. That is another of those crushing expectations we often place on ourselves. Rather, we cry out—even babble—to God as we can. If you cannot speak, cry; if you cannot cry, groan; and if you cannot even groan to God, "let thy prayer be at least a breathing,— a vital, sincere desire, the outpouring of thine inner life in the simplest and weakest form, and God will accept it. In a word, when you cannot pray as you would, take care to pray as you can."[44]

As well as urging believers to strive against all that might discourage them to pray, Spurgeon recommended two great aids for those struggling in prayer: (1) the blood of Christ and (2) the glory of Christ.

The blood of Christ is God's guarantee that he will hear the prayers of his children. Not only is God a faithful God who cannot lie, who promises to answer those who call on him (Ps. 50:15; Zech. 13:9), but the cross definitively *proves* his love and faithfulness toward his people. "You misread Calvary," Spurgeon assured his people, "if you think that prayer is useless."[45] Christians, therefore, should always have an eye on the blood of Christ whenever they pray: it will both assure and inflame their prayer.

The glory of Christ is, then, the guiding light for believers in prayer. Not only does the beauty and majesty of Christ inspire worship and praise in every Christian heart; the glory of Christ also *directs* and *shapes* Christian prayer. When Christians pray with an eye to Christ's glory, the selfish and petty requests they would present are outshone by a brighter and greater ambition. When we contemplate the glory of God in the face of Christ, we find ourselves moved to pray for *Christ's* cause on earth over our own.[46]

The blood of Christ assures us as we pray, and the glory of Christ draws us to more godly—indeed, more *glorious*—praying.

---

44 "Comfort for Those Whose Prayers Are Feeble," in *MTP*, 54:124.
45 "The Golden Key of Prayer," in *MTP*, 11:149–50.
46 "Pray for Jesus," in *MTP*, 12:589–600.

CHAPTER 10

THE PILGRIM ARMY

Two of Spurgeon's favorite books were by John Bunyan: *The Pilgrim's Progress* and *The Holy War*; and together they represent two key aspects of the Christian life as Spurgeon saw it.

After the Bible, *The Pilgrim's Progress* was almost certainly the book that sunk deepest into Spurgeon's being. He read it over a hundred times in his life and quoted it frequently in his sermons. An inscribed copy of *The Pilgrim's Progress* is what he would present to the young Miss Susannah Thompson shortly before declaring his love and proposing to her.[1] It is not surprising, then, that pilgrimage imagery and the idea of the Christian life as a pilgrimage to the Celestial City should feature so prominently in his thought and his sermons. The very name of Spurgeon's church—The Metropolitan *Tabernacle*—captured the sense of a pilgrim people on their way through the wilderness of the world. Pilgrimage, Spurgeon believed,

> is one of the leading ideas of Christianity. Every Christian is mystically a pilgrim. His rest is not here. He is not a citizen of earth. Here he has no abiding city. He journeys to a shrine unseen by mortal eye, whither his fathers have arrived. This life-journey is his one incessant occupation. He came into the world that he might march through it in haste. He is ever a pilgrim, in the fullest and truest sense.[2]

---

[1] *Autobiog.*, 2:7.
[2] C. H. Spurgeon, *The Saint and His Savior: The Progress of the Soul in the Knowledge of Jesus* (New York: Sheldon, Blakeman & Co., 1858), 316.

In equal measure, Spurgeon's thought and language had a martial and chivalric color. For as much as Christians are pilgrims, they are soldiers in the ecclesial army of Christ. It is right for us to think of Christ's church, he taught, "as an army with banners, marching to the fray, to achieve victories for Christ, to storm the strongholds of the foe, and to add province after province to the Redeemer's kingdom."[3] As such, the new life to be had in Christ is not one of sloth and ease; it is one of keen resolution to follow Christ in his victorious war on darkness, each week making "some distinct inroad upon the territory of the archenemy."[4] Faithlessness he would thus often equate with cowardice.[5] Hear, then, the soldierly and heroic notes in his charge to his students:

> In the Name of the Lord, let us again set up our banner, the royal standard of Jesus the Crucified. Let us sound the trumpets joyously, and let us march on, not with the trembling footsteps of those who know that they are bent upon an enterprise of evil, but with the gallant bearing of men whose cause is Divine, whose warfare is a crusade. Courage, my brethren; behold, the angels of God fly in our front, and, lo, the eternal God Himself leads our van. "The Lord of hosts is with us; the God of Jacob is our refuge."[6]

Such stirring calls to arms were common in the ministry of Spurgeon, who often depicted the pastor as a captain in the army of the Lord of hosts. Elsewhere he could describe a minister pleading with an unbeliever as being like a great naval warship "lying side by side with an enemy's man-of-war and pouring in broadsides of red-hot shot."[7] Or he could tell preachers, "Regard your pulpit as your steed, and dash into the battle like Khaled of old, smiting right and left with dauntless valour."[8] But as with other things, Spurgeon's military rhetoric was not merely for public show: it was ingrained in the man, as his private diary shows. See, for example:

> April 27.—Fear, begone! Doubts, fall back! In the name of the Lord of hosts I would set up my banner. Come on, ye demons of the pit, my Captain is more than a match for you; in His name, armed with His weapons, and

---

[3] C. H. Spurgeon, *The Soul Winner: How to Lead Sinners to the Saviour* (New York: Fleming H. Revell, 1895), 203–4.
[4] *S&T: 1872*, 91.
[5] *ARM*, 28.
[6] *ARM*, 31.
[7] *S&T: 1872*, 92.
[8] *ARM*, 122.

in His strength, I dare defy you all. How glorious 'twould be to die by the side of such a Leader![9]

Or again, from a private letter: "May we be enabled to go on, brave as lions, and valiant for the truth and cause of King Jesus, and by the help of the Spirit, vow eternal warfare with every sin, and rest not until the sword of the Spirit has destroyed all the enemies in our hearts!"[10]

Manliness

It has been argued that the extent of all this soldierly language comes from nineteenth-century ideas of "muscular Christianity."[11] Certainly Spurgeon's language tended to be muscular. "God," he declared, "chooses not milksops, destitute of backbone, to wear his glory upon their faces."[12] And there was something distinctly Victorian about his love of manliness, constantly pitted as it was against what he saw as the flowery artifice of the High Church Oxford movement. When one of his students began a prayer with the words "O Thou that art encinctured with an auriferous zodiac"(!), he took the grandiloquence as a sure sign (later justified) that the man had little Christian integrity.[13] Christians should not be affected or pretentious in their manners or speech, preachers especially.

> Well did Cicero exhort orators to adopt their gestures rather from the camp or the wrestling ring than from the dancers with their effeminate niceties. Manliness must never be sacrificed to elegance. Our working classes will never be brought even to consider the truth of Christianity by teachers who are starched and fine.[14]

Yet it would be simplistic, even misleading, to see Spurgeon's martial and muscular language as a mere product of the nineteenth-century "muscular Christianity" movement. For one thing, it could as well be considered the mark of Bunyan on him, or something of the robustness of Luther in him. And it was not as if he ever advocated self-involved machismo.

---

9 *Autobiog.*, 1:133.
10 C. H. Spurgeon, *The Letters of Charles Haddon Spurgeon* (London: Marshall Brothers, 1923), 49.
11 A. Bradstock, "'A Man of God Is a Manly Man': Spurgeon, Luther and 'Holy Boldness,'" in *Masculinity and Spirituality in Victorian Culture*, ed. A. Bradstock, S. Gill, A. Horgan, and S. Morgan (Basingstoke, England: Macmillan, 2000), 212–13.
12 *MTP*, 36:257.
13 *Autobiog.*, 2:152.
14 *Lectures*, 2:196.

Machismo is a distorted, cartoonish caricature of the human flourishing of manhood Spurgeon promoted. What he longed to see was more strength exercised (and restrained) in the name of love for Christ. In other words, he wanted believers to have a backbone to their faith. As he put it to his students:

> We have too many in our company who will go right if they are led aright, and who are sure to swim in the right direction if the current is strong enough to carry them with it; these are all very well when the wind blows from the right quarter, but they are of small use in ill weather. At this hour, there is a call for men who can breast the torrent, and swim up stream. We need heroes who would just as soon go alone, if necessary, as march with a thousand comrades. We need men who are doing their own thinking, and do not put it out, as families do with their washing. They have thought out the truth; and, having gone to God about it, and felt the power of it in their own souls, they are not now to be moved from the hope of their calling. They are pillars in the house of our God, abiding in their places; and not mere caterpillars, crawling after something to eat. We need captains for the good ship who know their longitude and latitude, and can tell whence they came, and to what port they are steering. Our Commander needs warriors true as steel for this hour of conflict.[15]

But that call for men of courageous and sturdy faith does not mean Spurgeon would tolerate self-regarding and insensitive bearishness—or unapproachable loners. Quite the opposite. The people, he said,

> need men who can feel,—men of heart, weak and feeble men, who can sympathize with the timid and sorrowful. It is a blessed thing if a minister can weep his way into men's souls, or even stammer a path into their hearts. So, brethren, do not be afraid of being weak, but rejoice to be able to say, with the apostle, "When I am weak, then am I strong" [2 Cor. 12:10].[16]

Activism

More important than manliness, the thought that Christians are both pilgrims and soldiers meant that Spurgeon believed in eager activism as an essential ingredient of new life. A living faith will be abundant in

---

[15] *ARM*, 391.
[16] *ARM*, 221.

good works.[17] This is part of what he understood by our being "quick-ened" by Christ: we are given not simply a new *existence* in Christ but a *life*, which means *vitality*. And since we have been given this life, we must, Spurgeon argued, "live with all the possible energy of life."[18] That, after all, is characteristic of the life of Christ himself, who was never slothful nor ever lived for his own comfort. Thus it is that we grow in "our sense of oneness to Christ" when we live all out for him, for "then I get to read the heart of Him whose flowing tears, and bloody sweat, and dying wounds showed how much He loved poor fallen mankind."[19] And the thought of enjoying Christ more through sharing in his mission was a strong motivation for Spurgeon himself: "I delight in working for my Lord and Master," he said, "because I feel a blessed community of inter-est with Him."[20]

Bright—one might even say gleeful—activism certainly character-ized Spurgeon's life. On top of his preaching and pastoral ministry, he established and oversaw a host of ministries, including the Pastors' Col-lege, the Stockwell Orphanage, seventeen almshouses for poor and el-derly women, the Colportage Association, and a day school for children.[21] He was involved in the planting of 187 churches (94 in London or nearby, 43 in the southeast, 19 in the north of England). "God sparing my life," he once wrote, "if I have my people at my back, I will not rest until the dark county of Surrey is covered with places of worship."[22] Then there was the Evangelists' Association, established in 1863 to put on services in mission halls, chapels, and the open air. Within fifteen years there were five permanent missions, and hundreds of meetings were being held every year.

None of that is yet to have mentioned his books. Temperamentally, Spurgeon was impatient in his energy, and he chafed at having to sit in his study writing.

> It is a delight, a joy, a rapture, to talk out my thoughts in words that flash upon the mind at the instant when they are required; but it is poor drudg-ery to sit still, and groan for thoughts and words without succeeding in

---

17 *ARM*, 30.
18 "Pray for Jesus," in *MTP*, 12:600.
19 *Autobiog.*, 1:179.
20 *ARM*, 88.
21 See *S&T: 1884*, 151.
22 *Autobiog.*, 2:329.

obtaining them. Well may a man's books be called his "works," for, if every mind were constituted as mine is, it would be work indeed to produce a quarto volume.[23]

His very restlessness, however, inclined him to "leap at difficulties, and find them vanish or turn to triumphs,"[24] and he usually managed to compose material with impressive speed. On just one rainy day during a holiday in France, for example, he managed to write out a month's worth of daily meditations.[25]

While Spurgeon was an activist in his own inimitable way, he was adamant that Christian activism was the fruit of his theology, not simply his temperament.

> A Christian sluggard! Is there such a being? A *Christian* man on half time? A Christian man working not at all for his Lord; how shall I speak of him? *Time* does not tarry, DEATH does not tarry, HELL does not tarry; Satan is not lazy, all the powers of darkness are busy: how is it that you and I can be sluggish, if the Master has put us into his vineyard? Surely we must be void of understanding if, after being saved by the infinite love of God, we do not spend and be spent in his service. The eternal fitness of things demands that a saved man should be an earnest man.[26]

The Christian life is one of sharing the self-giving life of God. It must then be a proactively generous life committed to blessing others. And it is then that we experience more richly God's own joy.

More specifically, Spurgeon saw this as part of the sweet and light burden of Christ given to preachers. "I found," he said, "that I derived greater benefit by proclaiming to others what I had learned than if I had kept it all to myself."[27] The task of preaching, he found, was a burden for him, a mental and emotional load that often weighed very heavily on him, sometimes nearly overwhelming him. Yet, for all that, he confessed,

> I would sooner have my work to do than any other under the sun. Preaching Jesus Christ is sweet work, joyful work, Heavenly work. Whitefield used to call his pulpit his throne, and those who know the bliss of forget-

---

23 *Autobiog.*, 2:166.
24 *Autobiog.*, 1:206.
25 *Autobiog.*, 4:310.
26 C. H. Spurgeon, *Farm Sermons* (New York: Passmore & Alabaster, 1882), 18.
27 *Autobiog.*, 1:204.

ting everything beside the glorious, all-absorbing topic of Christ crucified, will bear witness that the term was aptly used.[28]

Spurgeon could be disconcertingly strong in his repeated calls for
Christians to be diligent and industrious in their labor for Christ. We are
simply not being faithful stewards, he maintained, if we are lazy. "I like
Adam Clarke's precept: 'Kill yourselves with work, and then pray yourselves alive again.' We shall never do our duty either to God or man if we are
sluggards."[29] When he was told that he was breaking down his constitution
with so much relentless work, he replied:

> Well, if I have done so, I am glad of it. I would do the same again. If I had
> fifty constitutions I would rejoice to break them down in the service of
> the Lord Jesus Christ. . . . Crowd as much as you can into every day, and
> postpone no work till to-morrow.[30]

> The zeal of God's house ate up our Master, and it is but a small matter if
> it consume his servants. If by excessive labour we die before reaching
> the average age of man, worn out in the Master's service, then, glory be
> to God, we shall have so much less of earth and so much more of heaven.[31]

That said, though, he believed it equally possible for Christians to over-
load themselves sinfully, and would warn them against so working as if the
salvation of the world depended upon themselves. The burden Christ lays
upon us is ultimately his own, and we are not being faithful stewards if we
imagine ourselves as ultimately significant. We are responsible before God,
but "you are not God, and you do not stand in God's place; you are not the
rulers of providence, and you have not been elected sole managers of the
covenant of grace; therefore do not act as if you were."[32]

Yet, Spurgeon would explain, the difference between faithful diligence
and idolatrous self-regard is not some fine balance we must tread. It is the
difference between faithful dependence on God and faithless self-reliance.
If Christians continually give out of their own finite resources, they must
eventually empty themselves out. We can be continuously fruitful only
insofar as we abide in Christ and feed on him. Therefore, "the most needful

---

[28] *Autobiog.*, 2:165.
[29] *ARM*, 272.
[30] *MTP*, 22:45.
[31] *S&T: 1877*, 81.
[32] *ARM*, 215.

and profitable labour is that which we spend upon our own mental and spiritual improvement. Whatever you do, take heed unto yourselves, and to your doctrine."[33] Faithful, fruitful activism flows only from a constant and enjoyed communion with Christ through his Word and prayer.

True Activism Is a Matter of the Heart

That being the case, Spurgeon was no advocate of the sort of spiritually hollow activism that concerns itself only with outward behavior. That would run entirely against his understanding that our new *life* comes from having a new *heart*. In fact, the transformed heart is the very reason for the enthusiasm of the Christian to be active and fruitful. Faithful activism for Christ is a manifestation of affections that have been reordered to share Christ's passions. Thus Spurgeon held that earnest zeal for the glory of God is the most essential quality in a Christian minister. It is the motor of Christian fruitfulness. Indeed, he believed, it is the secret of success:

> As a rule, real success is proportionate to the preacher's earnestness. Both great men and little men succeed if they are thoroughly alive unto God, and fail if they are not so. . . . In many instances ministerial success is traceable almost entirely to an intense zeal, a consuming passion for souls, and an eager enthusiasm in the cause of God, and we believe that in every case, other things being equal, men prosper in the divine service in proportion as their hearts are blazing with holy love.[34]

Only with such heartfelt love for God can the Christian truly share the life of Christ, who was consumed by zeal for God's house (John 2:17). Only that way can they be faithful and resolute for him.[35] Only that way can they be most truly joyous and *alive*, for to "live entirely for the Lord is to live indeed, all else is mere existing."[36]

---

[33] *ARM*, 262.

[34] *Lectures*, 2:215–16.

[35] "There was perhaps another reason for our Saviour's wonderful composure when he was attacked with stones, namely, that *his heart was so set upon his work* that he could not be turned away from it whatever the unbelieving Jews might do. . . . Happy is that man whom God has launched like a thunderbolt from his hand, who must go on and fulfil his destiny; happy that it is his vocation to bring sinners to the Saviour's feet. O blessed Spirit, lift us up to dwell in God, and so to sympathize with his fatherly compassion that we may heed neither stones, nor sneers, nor slanders, but become absorbed in our self-denying service for Jesus' sake!" (*MTP*, 29:674–75).

[36] *S&T: 1876*, 4.

CHAPTER 11

SUFFERING AND DEPRESSION

Charles Spurgeon was a man who crackled with life. Twinkle-eyed and fizzing with energy, he had a personality that still blazes through his works. It can therefore come as a bit of a surprise to find out how much Spurgeon suffered—and with depression. It shouldn't, of course: being full of life in a fallen world must mean distress, and Spurgeon's life was indeed full of physical and mental pain.

Aged twenty-two, as pastor of a large church and with twin babies at home to look after, he was preaching to thousands in the Surrey Gardens Music Hall when pranksters yelled "fire," starting a panic to exit the building which killed seven and left twenty-eight severely injured. His mind was never the same again. His wife, Susannah, wrote, "My beloved's anguish was so deep and violent, that reason seemed to totter in her throne, and we sometimes feared that he would never preach again."[1]

Then, from the age of thirty-three, physical pain became a large and constant feature of life for him. He suffered from a burning kidney inflammation called Bright's Disease, as well as gout, rheumatism, and neuritis. The pain was such that it soon kept him from preaching for one third of the time. Added to that, overwork, stress, and guilt about the stress began to take their toll. And all this was in the public eye and was jumped on by

[1] Charles Ray, "The Life of Susannah Spurgeon," in *Morning Devotions by Susannah Spurgeon: Free Grace and Dying Love* (Edinburgh: Banner of Truth, 2006), 166.

his many critics, not making it easier to bear. The suffering, they argued rather predictably, was a judgment from God. Spurgeon noted in *The Sword and Trowel*: "A clergyman writes to inform us that the gout is sent to us as a judgment from God for opposing the Church of England. If a swollen leg proves that a man is under God's displeasure, what would a broken neck prove? We ask the question with special reference to the late Bishop of Oxford."[2]

The pain, the politics, the opposition, and the overwork (as well as bereavements, like that of his young grandson) all affected him deeply, if in waves. So much so that today he would almost certainly be diagnosed as clinically depressed and treated with medication and therapy. The depression could hit him so intensely that, he once said, "I could say with Job, 'My soul chooseth strangling rather than life' [Job 7:15]. I could readily enough have laid violent hands upon myself, to escape from my misery of spirit."[3]

Sometimes, he confessed, "I become so perplexed that I sink in heart, and dream that it were better for me never to have been born than to have been called to bear all this multitude upon my heart."[4] Yet Spurgeon believed that God had a good purpose in all his suffering, and because of it felt he had become a better prepared and more compassionate pastor. It enabled him to deliver a striking and most unusual lecture to his students titled "The Minister's Fainting Fits," in which he said:

> Knowing by most painful experience what deep depression of spirit means, being visited therewith at seasons by no means few or far between, I thought it might be consolatory to some of my brethren if I gave my thoughts thereon, that younger men might not fancy that some strange thing had happened to them when they became for a season possessed by melancholy; and that sadder men might know that one upon whom the sun has shone right joyously did not always walk in the light.[5]

God's Purposes in Suffering

Before seeking relief from such melancholy, Spurgeon sought to understand God's purposes in these things that he might actually profit from the experience. It is quite clear from Scripture that through believers' suffering,

---

2 *S&T: 1874*, 123.
3 *MTP*, 36:200.
4 *S&T: 1881*, 177.
5 *Lectures*, 1:167.

God refines them like gold in a furnace (1 Pet. 1:6–7). Yet, Spurgeon wrote, "when the gold knows why and wherefore it is in the fire . . . [it] will thank the Refiner for putting it into the crucible, and will find a sweet satisfaction even in the flames."[6]

Spurgeon saw that our heavenly Father ordains suffering for believers. Though our trials may come from the world, the flesh, and the Devil, they are overruled and ordained by God, who treats them as an important part of our new life in Christ.[7] For a start, we simply could not be like Christ if we are not treated like him, if we have a life of ease when he had so much pain. "Do you expect to be crowned with gold where he was crowned with thorns? Shall lilies grow for you and briars for him?"[8]

The gods of other religions might give ease to the good and health to the worthy. Not so in Christianity, where "goodness" is Christ himself, and conformity to him. God will not therefore simply reward believers with ease in this life, for that would make ease, rather than Christ, the greater prize. Suffering is therefore a "covenant mark," a proof that God is our Father and therefore cares enough about us to do everything necessary to mold and clip us into the likeness of his happily holy Son. That, Spurgeon believed, was just why some, like Solomon, wander: because they have lacked the covenant mark of affliction.[9] Sinful unbelievers thus often enjoy prosperity and success in this life while the righteous are persecuted and suffer.[10]

This might all seem like bad news for the believer. After all, who wants to hurt? Yet, studying the lives of eminent men, Spurgeon came to the conclusion that those who never have to push through the waves of difficulty never grow in strength and maturity like those who do. Those who live in the lap of luxury and never experience the discipline of trouble tend always to be more frail and feeble in their faith. On the whole, therefore, "it is good for a man to bear the yoke; good for a man to breast the billows; good for a man to pass through fire and through water, and so to learn sublime lessons."[11] Trouble can strengthen, and trouble can reveal the work that needs to be done in us. In that sense our lives, Spurgeon explained, can be likened to a pool of water. When it is allowed to stand still and at ease for a

---

[6] *S&T: 1866*, 36.
[7] *MTP*, 38:2–3.
[8] *MTP*, 23:270.
[9] William Williams, *Personal Reminiscences of Charles Haddon Spurgeon* (London: Passmore & Alabaster, 1895), 73.
[10] *Autobiog.*, 2:216.
[11] *MTP*, 31:327–28.

while, it can look clean and pure, for all the mud has sunk out of sight to the bottom. Only when it is stirred and disturbed is the impurity revealed. Just so, trials show up our sins in how viciously and selfishly we react to them. Through them we get to know ourselves better, recognize the evils that had previously lain hidden in our hearts, and then fight them.[12] Therefore, Spurgeon said, "I fear me, there are very few of the godly who will fully ripen without affliction. The vine bears but little fruit unless it makes the acquaintance of the knife, and is sternly pruned."[13]

Being so fruitful himself, he knew of what he spoke. Had he not often been brought so low, he felt that the extraordinary fruitfulness of his ministry would have been the ruin of him.[14]

> Uninterrupted success and unfading joy in it would be more than our weak heads could bear. Our wine must needs be mixed with water, lest it turn our brains. My witness is, that those who are honoured of their Lord in public, have usually to endure a secret chastening, or to carry a peculiar cross, lest by any means they exalt themselves, and fall into the snare of the devil.[15]

Thus, he found, depression would often come over him before any period of special blessing on his ministry. Divine blessing would loom over him like a black cloud before breaking and yielding its shower of goodness. That was especially the case when he first came to London and found himself successful. Far from being elated at the thought of a career which he began to see would be extraordinarily abundant, he found himself emotionally crushed by the burden.[16] But that was vital, for the ministerial burden he would be called to carry was one that could be borne only by a humbled man.

Believers can also profit from suffering in other ways. Tears, Spurgeon discovered through experience, can clear the eye so that we see with an improved vision and perspective. Losses reveal the insufficiency of all the things around us that we cherish, enabling us to appreciate the all-sufficiency of Christ more.[17] For, just as we enjoy the stars better when it is dark, so when all is dark in life around us we can enjoy heavenly glories

---

12 *MTP*, 27:640.
13 *MTP*, 36:604.
14 *MTP*, 48:461.
15 *Lectures*, 1:178.
16 *Autobiog.*, 1:362.
17 *MTP*, 34:100.

better.[18] And not just heavenly ones. Times of sorrow can tenderize us to appreciate little, everyday, otherwise forgettable blessings.

> You know, dear brothers and sisters, how a little act of kindness will cheer us when we are very low in spirit. If we are despised and rejected of men, if we are deserted and defamed by those who ought to have dealt differently with us, even a tender look from a child will help to remove our depression. In times of loneliness, it is something even to have a dog with you, to lick your hand, and show you such kindness as is possible from him.[19]

Sorrows not only enable us to appreciate blessings from the Lord; they throw us onto him. Fear and tribulation make us cling to him as times of comfort never would: "When you and I were little boys, and we were out at eventide walking with our father, we used sometimes to run on a long way ahead; but, by-and-by, there was a big dog loose on the road, and it is astonishing how closely we clung to our father then."[20] All told, said Spurgeon, the "rod of God teacheth us more than all the voices of his ministers."[21] Strong words indeed from one with so high a view of preaching!

Being a pastor, he was sensitively aware of *how* to give such theology to people who are in the throes of pain. The ways a believer can profit from suffering cannot be trotted out coolly to those who are reeling and weeping. There is a time simply to sit and weep with them. And yet, he found, there is for all believers, regardless of their emotional state, a wonderful comfort to be found in knowing God's Fatherly providence. To a couple who had recently lost their child he felt he could write this note:

> Dear Friend,—
>
> I beseech our Lord to minister comfort both to you and your sorrowing wife. It must be a very severe stroke to you, and it is a sign that our Father loves you very much and thinks a great deal of you. I had a watch once which I allowed to lie at ease and never worried it with cleaning for I thought it worthless; but one which keeps time to a second gets wound up every night with a key which touches its inmost springs, and sometimes it gets taken to pieces—for it is worth it.[22]

---

[18] *MTP*, 49:249.
[19] *MTP*, 48:115.
[20] *MTP*, 48:462.
[21] *MTP*, 22:76.
[22] C. H. Spurgeon, *The Letters of Charles Haddon Spurgeon* (London: Marshall Brothers, 1923), 170.

As well as hearing of God's loving and mighty Fatherliness, Christians in the midst of suffering often need to hear of how suffering is a covenant mark. Naturally we are quick to take suffering to mean that God is against us or has somehow weakened in his love and care for us. That is not so. "Depression of spirit is no index of declining grace; the very loss of joy and the absence of assurance may be accompanied by the greatest advancement in the spiritual life."[23] We should therefore not be too easily dismayed by our troubles: in a failing world, friends will fail us, we will hurt, and we will feel our frailty and emptiness. But none of that is any indication that our Father has forgotten or failed us, nor that we might no longer be useful.

God Uses Pastors Who Suffer

If trials can be beneficial for all believers, they are invaluable for gospel ministers. When pastors preach from a broken heart, they can often relate far better to the despairing and thus offer a deeper consolation.[24] When a pastor patiently endures difficulty and affliction, and keeps rejoicing in God, it powerfully commends the gospel as glad tidings of great joy.[25] The pastor—or, indeed, any Christian who ministers to another—can prove the comfort that is to be found in God in such times. God therefore often leads his under-shepherds through trials, "not so much for their own benefit as for the sake of those to whom they may afterwards minister."[26]

Spurgeon knew that pastoring is normally slow work. Troubled people "cannot be dismissed with just a word of hope and a dose of medicine, but require a long time in which to tell their griefs and to receive their comfort."[27] After all,

> Whoever sings songs to a heavy heart
> > is like one who takes off a garment on a cold day,
> > and like vinegar on soda. (Prov. 25:20)

That being the case, pastors need to develop the compassion of the Man of Sorrows, and that normally takes suffering to develop. Certainly that was how it was for Spurgeon himself: through experiencing depression, he said,

---

23 *MTP*, 48:461.
24 *ARM*, 63.
25 "Joy, a Duty," in *MTP*, 41:136.
26 *MTP*, 18:217.
27 *MTP*, 38:51.

"I have learnt from it to be very tender with all fellow-sufferers."[28] It is a difficult thing for a man who has had a life of ease and comfort

> to sympathize with another whose path has been exceedingly rough;
> even though that successful man should try to sympathize, he does it
> very awkwardly. . . . "Stuff and nonsense!" says a strong man to some poor
> suffering one; "you are too nervous; try and exert yourself." That is often
> one of the most cruel things that can be said to the sufferer. But if the
> man has been through a similar experience, he uses another tone of voice
> altogether.[29]

Christian ministers should therefore expect a special degree of suffering to be given to them as a way of forming them for Christlike, compassionate ministry. Christ himself was made like his weak and tempted brothers in order that he might help those who are tempted (Heb. 2:16–18), and in the same manner, it is weak and suffering people that God has chosen to minister to the weak and suffering. Angels or supermen simply could not sympathize with human groans; their very strength would only mock our weakness and thus mock the gospel.[30] Spurgeon therefore tended to put his trust more in those ministers who exhibited joy and peace in God while *having been dragged through particular suffering*.[31] Indeed, he said,

> if you have never had such an experience, my dear brother, you will not
> be worth a pin as a preacher. You cannot help others who are depressed
> unless you have been down in the depths yourself. You cannot lift others
> out of despondency and depression, unless you yourself have sometimes
> need to be lifted out of such experiences. You must be compassed with
> this infirmity, too, at times, in order to have compassion on those in a
> similar case.[32]

Wisdom on Coping: Physical Remedies

Through his own experience, Spurgeon developed an appreciation of the complexity of the human mind and some of the reasons for its ill-health. His doctor drew a connection between his kidney complaint and his

---

28 *MTP*, 48:525.
29 *MTP*, 54:375.
30 *Lectures*, 1:168.
31 *Lectures*, 2:81–82.
32 *MTP*, 38:180.

mental state, believing that mental causes and overwork exacerbated his physical suffering. At the same time, Spurgeon came to see that he was much more prone to depression when physically ill. As such, he saw that while gloomy despondency *can* be bound up with sinful habits of mind, it is not so simple. In some, he said, *"it is rather their disease than their sin, and more their misfortune than their fault."*[33] For *"some persons are constitutionally sad. . . . [They] have bad livers, feeble digestions, or irritated brains."*[34] And this can be true of even the godliest Christian:

> We do not profess that the religion of Christ will so thoroughly change a man as to take away from him all his natural tendencies; it will give the despairing something that will alleviate that despondency, but as long as that is caused by a low state of body, or a diseased mind, we do not profess that the religion of Christ will totally remove it.[35]

Spurgeon could also observe the flip side of that: the abundant faith and joy of some Christians is only because they have enjoyed lives of more undisturbed ease.

> There are a great many of you who appear to have a large stock of faith, but it is only because you are in very good health and your business is prospering. If you happened to get a disordered liver, or your business should fail, I should not be surprised if nine parts out of ten of your wonderful faith should evaporate. . . . Let a man have a bad headache for about half an hour, and let him see whether he does not feel himself to be mortal, and to have something sinful about him still.[36]

Physical infirmities, opposition, bereavements: all can cause mental suffering as much as sin and guilt. Indeed, "after extraordinary exaltations," he noted from experience, "it often happens that God's servants are greatly depressed."[37] But perhaps more than anything else, for Spurgeon himself it was the unrelenting burden of gospel ministry—with all its rigor, disappointments, and frustrations—that wore him down and made him so prone to depression. "All mental work tends to weary and to depress, for much study is a weariness of the flesh; but ours is more than mental

---

33 *MTP*, 16:269.
34 *MTP*, 36:297.
35 *NPSP*, 5:145–46.
36 *MTP*, 51:351.
37 *MTP*, 14:188.

work—it is heart work, the labour of our inmost soul. How often, on Lord's-day evenings, do we feel as if life were completely washed out of us!"[38]

That being the case, Spurgeon sought a number of *physical* remedies to alleviate his *mental* despondency. From 1871 he sought each winter to escape the darkness, cold, and dirt of London by retreating to Mentone, on the French Riviera. There he found in the balmy warmth and the light a natural reviver for body and mind. And when he couldn't make it that far, he found a simple walk in the countryside would help.

> A day's breathing of fresh air upon the hills, or a few hours' ramble in the beech woods' umbrageous calm, would sweep the cobwebs out of the brain of scores of our toiling ministers who are now but half alive. A mouthful of sea air, or a stiff walk in the wind's face, would not give grace to the soul, but it would yield oxygen to the body, which is next best.[39]

Spurgeon used similar restorative language when he wrote of "smoking to the glory of God." For him, cigars were an acceptable and agreeable means of relaxation when life was otherwise overwhelming. "I have felt grateful to God," he wrote to the *Daily Telegraph*, when "I have found intense pain relieved, a weary brain soothed, and calm, refreshing sleep obtained by a cigar."[40]

And, in some tension with his exhortations that Christians should burn out for Jesus, he held that relaxing rest is essential if Christians are to stay strong and fresh for the long haul of life.

> The bow cannot be always bent without fear of breaking. Repose is as needful to the mind as sleep to the body. . . . Hence the wisdom and compassion of our Lord, when he said to his disciples, "Let us go into the desert and rest awhile." . . . The Master knows better than to exhaust his servants and quench the light of Israel. Rest time is not waste time. It is economy to gather fresh strength.[41]

Wisdom on Coping: Turning to God

As well as recommending such physical palliatives for the mental sufferer, Spurgeon urged patient carefulness in making any assessment of the situ-

---

[38] *Lectures*, 1:170.
[39] *Lectures*, 1:172.
[40] Letter to the *Daily Telegraph* (September 23, 1874), cited in Lewis A. Drummond, *Spurgeon: Prince of Preachers* (Grand Rapids: Kregel, 1992), 506.
[41] *Lectures*, 1:174.

ation. He knew how quick we are to assume, when set back and depressed, that grace has left us, or that we have become pointless. Thus he advised:

> Just now, when anguish fills the heart, and the spirits are bruised with sore pain and travail, it is not the best season for forming a candid judgment of our own condition, or of anything else; let the judging faculty lie by, and let us with tears of loving confession throw ourselves upon our Father's bosom, and looking up into his face believe that he loves us with all his infinite heart.[42]

In such times, instead of seeking a definite understanding of the "what" and the "why" of our situation, we should simply hold fast to God's promises. Having at all times an objective truth that does not depend on our ability to *feel* their truth, the promises of God are like a light that cannot be overcome by our darkness. They are an immovable and infinite comfort beyond the reach of our finite trouble and doubt. It was for that reason that Susannah Spurgeon had Matthew 5:11–12 framed for them to see every day in their bedroom: "Blessed are ye, when men shall revile you, and persecute you, and shall say all manner of evil against you falsely, for my sake. Rejoice, and be exceeding glad: for great is your reward in heaven: for so persecuted they the prophets which were before you" (KJV).

The matter of perspective—God's sovereignty and our creatureliness—was essential to how Spurgeon himself coped. Many Christians, he knew, wear themselves out through an oppressive sense of responsibility. Seeking to be successful, they take the burden of the universe upon their shoulders and buckle under it. Spurgeon felt this temptation with all his pastoral duties and church plants, with the orphans and widows he provided for, and with the constant fundraising necessary for his Pastors' College. Yet, when once asked, "Do not these responsibilities come upon you sometimes with a kind of crushing weight?" Spurgeon answered, "No: the Lord is a good banker, I trust him. He has never failed me. Why should I be anxious?"[43]

For Spurgeon, enjoying God's lordship was not an *inactive* knowledge of that truth, though. He would take comfort in God's promises and kind sovereignty, but he would also *plead* them. In times of pain and distress he

---

[42] *S&T: 1876*, 66.
[43] Wayland Hoyt, *Walks and Talks with Charles H. Spurgeon* (Philadelphia: American Baptist Publication Society, 1892), 10.

would turn to God in prayer and beg him to prove his Fatherly care. Those caught in a black cloud of depression might well feel that such bold prayer is just what they don't feel up to. They feel lackluster and worthless, not audacious. Yet, to the depressed who saw their own unworthiness as a bar to prayer, he said:

> In your most depressed seasons you are to get joy and peace through believing. "Ah!" says one, "but suppose you have fallen into some great sin— what then?" Why then the more reason that you should cast yourself upon him. Do you think Jesus Christ is only for little sinners? Is he a doctor that only heals finger-aches? Beloved, it is no faith to trust Christ when I have not any sin, but it is true faith when I am foul, and black, and filthy; when during the day I have tripped up and fallen, and done serious damage to my joy and peace, to go back again to that dear fountain and say, "Lord, I never loved washing so much before as I do to-night, for to-day I have made a fool of myself; I have said and done what I ought not to have done, and I am ashamed and full of confusion, but I believe Christ can save me, even me, and I will rest in him still."[44]

Wisdom on Coping: Finding Comfort in Christ

When ministering to the downcast, pastors commonly point people to the resurrection and the victory of Christ. And the thought of death defeated, tears wiped away, and exchanging the helmets and swords of our struggle for palm branches and crowns was all essential comfort for Spurgeon. However, when pastoring the suffering and depressed, he seemed most often to have focused people on Christ crucified and as the Man of Sorrows. For, he said, the afflicted "do not so much look for comfort to Christ as he will come a second time in splendour of state, as to Christ as he came the first time, a weary man and full of woes."[45] Where Jesus in his heavenly glory might seem too exalted for the emotionally battered to approach, Jesus in his pain-racked humility can be just the balm they need. Spurgeon found for himself that in seasons of great pain, the "sympathy of Jesus is the next most precious thing to his sacrifice."[46] Again and again Spurgeon therefore returned to the theme of Christ's compassion for his suffering people. In an 1890 sermon titled "The Tenderness of Jesus," for example, he spoke, while

---

44 *MTP*, 12:298–99.
45 *MTP*, 19:121–22.
46 *MTP*, 19:124–25. Cf. *NPSP*, 1, sermon 35.

feeling his own weakness, about Christ as the High Priest who feels for us in our infirmities. "This morning," he said,

> being myself more than usually compassed with infirmities, I desire to speak, as a weak and suffering preacher, of that High Priest who is full of compassion: and my longing is that any who are low in spirit, faint, despondent, and even out of the way, may take heart to approach the Lord Jesus. . . .
>
> . . . Jesus is touched, not with a feeling of your strength, but of your infirmity. Down here, poor, feeble nothings affect the heart of their great High Priest on high, who is crowned with glory and honour. As the mother feels with the weakness of her babe, so does Jesus feel with the poorest, saddest, and weakest of his chosen.[47]

In suffering, then, it is not only the case that we get to draw nearer to Christ, becoming more like him and leaning more fully on him. In such times Christ draws near to us to walk with his people in the furnace. And not only to walk with us, but to bear us through.

> In the old *Pilgrim's Progress* I used to read in my grandfather's house, I remember the picture of Hopeful in the river holding Christian up; and the engraver has done it very well. Hopeful has his arm round Christian, and lifts up his hands, and says, "Fear not, brother, I feel the bottom." That is just what Jesus does in our trials; he puts his arm round us, points up, and says, "Fear not! the water may be deep, but the bottom is good."[48]

And, Christ being the "happy God," his nearness with us in such times will instill a sweetness into the bitterness of suffering. Indeed, that is his ultimate purpose even in the darkness: to share more of that joy which one day we will have beyond all contamination.

---

[47] *MTP*, 36:315, 320.
[48] *MTP*, 44:202.

CHAPTER 12

FINAL GLORY

The Christian Life Is a Hopeful Life

Spurgeon's was a Christ-centered theology, meaning that since Christ is now in heaven, Christians must look there and long for his return. Our faith and very lives are stimulated and shaped by the fact that *"our position towards our Lord is that of waiting for His coming."*[1] Christians, in other words, are hopeful, not in the sense that they hope for some *event* as such; their hope is, above all, to enjoy the undiluted *presence of Christ.*

The hope that Christians have is sure and certain. First, the Scriptures promise Christ's return: his work of resurrection must be finished, his victory over death and evil must be universally enforced. Second, Christian hope is certain because those who have been united to Christ in his death and resurrection "cannot be lost. Lost? Impossible! For who is able to snatch us out of our Father's hand [John 10:29]?"[2] Clothed in the righteousness of Christ, saints are held safe by God for the day of Christ's coming, and may hope for it unreservedly and with absolute confidence.[3]

When he returns, he will judge and destroy all wickedness, purifying his creation. That means we may look forward to the end of all tears and grief. In particular, Spurgeon often held out to the bereaved the hope that we will meet our loved ones again. To one who had recently lost his daughter, he wrote:

---

[1] *ARM*, 389.
[2] C. H. Spurgeon, *The Letters of Charles Haddon Spurgeon* (London: Marshall Brothers, 1923), 49.
[3] *MTP*, 17:384.

MENTONE, *Dec.* 14, '87
DEAR MR. BARTLETT,—

I sorrow with you over the departure of your little Lillie; but you will feel that there is honey with the gall. She was a dear child ready to take her place with the shining ones. Grandmother will receive her as a messenger from you.

May peace and consolation flow into the heart of yourself and wife. I send you a little cheque to ease the expense. I cannot ease your pain but there is "another Comforter" Who can and will do so. Receive my hearty sympathy. We are all going the same way. The little one has outrun us; we shall catch her up soon.

Yours very heartily,
        C. H. SPURGEON.[4]

Spurgeon clearly saw that the Christian hope is to enjoy both communion with God and communion with the people of God. "Jerusalem the golden is the place of *communion* with all the people of God. We shall sit with Abraham, Isaac, and Jacob, in eternal fellowship. . . . We shall not sing solos, but in chorus shall we praise our King."[5] The fact that Revelation speaks of there being no more sea Spurgeon took symbolically to mean "there will be no *division*." Where now the sea divides people from people, when Christ returns there will be universal and constant harmony, with no fear of any "storm to wreck our hopes and drown our joys."[6]

A Christ-Centered Hope

What clearly stood at the heart of Spurgeon's hope, though—and loomed large there!—was the person of Christ. While Christians long for an end to all fallenness and injustice, and for perfected communion with other believers, Christ is central.

Oh, to think of heaven without Christ! It is the same thing as thinking of hell. Heaven without Christ! It is day without the sun; existing without life, feasting without food, seeing without light. It involves a contradic-

---

[4] Spurgeon, *The Letters of Charles Haddon Spurgeon*, 168–69.
[5] Charles H. Spurgeon, *Morning and Evening: Daily Readings*, complete and unabridged, new modern ed. (Peabody, MA: Hendrickson, 2006), evening, July 12. Cf. *MTP*, 8:172.
[6] Spurgeon, *Morning and Evening*, evening, December 19.

tion in terms. Heaven without Christ! Absurd. It is the sea without water, the earth without its fields, the heavens without their stars. There cannot be heaven without Christ. He is the sum total of bliss; the fountain from which heaven flows, the element of which heaven is composed. Christ is heaven and heaven is Christ. You shall change the words and make no difference in the sense. To be where Jesus is is the highest imaginable bliss, and bliss away from Jesus is inconceivable to the child of God.[7]

Heaven is heavenly precisely because it is the place of communion with Christ, where his glory is enjoyed. And hell is hellish because it is the place of cast-out Christlessness—"for it is hell for you to depart from Christ."[8] None of this should be misconstrued: we have seen already that Spurgeon's robust Christ-centeredness was a clearly and fully *Trinitarian* Christ-centeredness. The Father and the Spirit were not ignored. Yet for Spurgeon it was primarily the presence or absence of Christ that makes for the joy or the horror of our eternal destiny. It is the presence of Christ that makes all the goodness of heaven abound; in his absence there is nothing but withering darkness and the unrestrained wrath of God toward evil.

Spurgeon had a strong fear that the eternal beauties and joys that Christ offers might eclipse Christ himself in the desires and affections of our hearts. He therefore became quite uncomfortable when Christians spoke of all the wonders of the new creation we shall get to enjoy. Some would wax lyrical about how we shall one day explore the depths of science, our minds freed from sin to fathom mysteries of creation now closed to us. In contrast, he said, "I will sit down, and look at Jesus. . . . There will be little else we shall want of heaven beside Jesus Christ."[9] His teaching, therefore, did not tend to linger on the *redemption* of God's creation or on creation or new creation as a vehicle and mirror of God's glory. He would teach the bodily resurrection of both the righteous and the wicked, but his emphasis was on the physical creation as something that could almost be discarded if thereby we might *instead* enjoy the spiritual.[10]

God's great new-creating work ought to fill us with such joy as to make us forget the old creation, as though we said to ourselves:—What are the

---

7 *MTP*, 19:570–71.
8 *ARM*, 145.
9 *MTP*, 47:617–18.
10 "The Resurrection of the Dead," in *NPSP*, 2:97–107.

sun and the moon? We shall not have need of these variable lights in
the perfection of the new creation, for in heaven, "They need no candle,
neither light of the sun" [Rev. 22:5]. What is the sea, though it be the
very mirror of beauty? In that new creation there will be no more sea,
and storms, and tempests will be all unknown. What are these luxu-
ries of sight and hearing? We shall not want them when our eyes shall
behold the King in his beauty in the land that is very far off. The joy
of the spiritual is such that, while it admits the joy of the natural, yet,
nevertheless, it swallows it up as Aaron's rod swallowed up the rods of
the magicians [Ex. 7:12].[11]

Spurgeon's strong concentration on Christ also made him chary of
spending much time on debated or speculative aspects of eschatology.
Not that he was ignorant of the various eschatological systems: he was
raised, as was typical for the time, as a postmillennialist and became a
premillennialist shortly after his move to London.[12] Yet his concern was
that the person of Christ—not the millennium or the date of Christ's return—should be central to the Christian's hope. And with Christ before
them, Christians should live in active hope, not sequestered debate or
theorizing.

Your guess at the number of the beast, your Napoleonic speculations,
your conjectures concerning a personal Antichrist—forgive me, I count
them but mere bones for dogs; while men are dying, and hell is filling, it
seems to me the veriest drivel to be muttering about an Armageddon at
Sebastopol or Sadowa or Sedan, and peeping between the folded leaves of
destiny to discover the fate of Germany.[13]

There are good brethren in the world who are impractical. The grand doctrine of the Second Advent makes them stand with open mouths, peering
into the skies, so that I am ready to say, "Ye men of Plymouth, why stand ye
here gazing up into Heaven?" The fact that Jesus Christ is to come again,
is not a reason for star-gazing, but for working in the power of the Holy
Ghost. Be not so taken up with speculations as to prefer a Bible-reading
over an obscure passage in the Revelation to teaching in a Ragged-school
or discoursing to the poor concerning Jesus.[14]

---

11 *MTP*, 37:353.
12 Contrast the postmillennial views found in *NPSP*, 1:235, with his premillennial statements found, for
example, in *MTP*, 32:195–96.
13 *Lectures*, 1:83.
14 *ARM*, 54.

The Glory of God

It seems fitting to finish this book with a brief look at Spurgeon on glory. For glory is not only the Christian's final destination; Spurgeon's theology of the Christian life was one compassed about on all sides by the glory of God. We have life and new life because of the glory of God, and the glory of God is what we live, hope, and aim for. It is our whence, our whither, our where, and our why.

The glory of God concerns the nature of God in all his manifold perfections: he is altogether and simply glorious in his holiness, his love, his righteousness, his justice, and so on. Yet, Spurgeon observed, when Moses asked to see God's glory, the Lord did not offer to show him his justice, holiness, wrath, or power, but offered to make all his *goodness* pass before him (Ex. 33:18–19). "Ah!" said Spurgeon, "*the goodness of God is God's glory. God's greatest glory is that he is good. The brightest gem in the crown of God is his goodness.*"[15] Elsewhere he could similarly say that *love* is "the prominent point of the divine character."[16] He did not, however, mean to exalt one attribute at the expense of another. He regarded God's love "in the high theological sense, in which, like a golden circle, it holds within itself all the divine attributes: for God were not love if he were not just, and did not hate every unholy thing."[17] Moreover, he taught that to proclaim God's loving goodness without his sovereignty would not completely set forth his nature.[18]

> Put the two together, goodness and sovereignty, and you see God's glory. If you take sovereignty alone, you will not understand God. Some people only have an idea of God's sovereignty, and not of his goodness; such are usually gloomy, harsh, and ill-humoured. You must put the two together; that God is good, and that God is a Sovereign. You must speak of sovereign grace. God is not gracious alone, he is sovereignly gracious. He is not sovereign alone, but he is graciously sovereign.[19]

The glory of the living God is a self-giving, fertile glory. He rejoices to give and share his eternal happiness and life, and he has proved this on the cross. "Do you not see the great unselfish glory of God in Christ Jesus?

---

15 *MTP*, 54:568.
16 *MTP*, 61:98.
17 *Lectures*, 2:271.
18 *MTP*, 54:569.
19 *MTP*, 54:571.

When did he ever live unto himself? What single act of his had a selfish purpose?"[20] The existence of all life and every part of creation is due to this superabundant characteristic of God's glory. They are the outflow of deity. "God has gone forth out of himself into the creation, and filled all things."[21] That is why, "if you ever get a vision of the glory of God in nature, and if you then turn your thoughts toward the Lord's Christ, you will see that the same God is in him as in the visible universe, and that the same glory shines in him, only more clearly."[22]

The outgoing, self-giving nature of God's glory is the reason for all created life, and it is the reason we have a gospel of grace. But there is a gracious undertow to God's expansive glory: as God in his glory gives *out*, so in that same glory he draws his creation *in* to enjoy his life-giving presence. And therein lies our hope: despite the fall, the creation he brought into being has a tendency

> towards him, to return, in fact, to him from whom it came. Is it not just so in the life of Christ? He seems to be drawing all things to himself, gathering together all things in one in his own personality. Some of these things will not move, but yet his attraction has fallen on them, while others fly with alacrity to him, according to his word, "I, if I be lifted up, will draw all men unto me" [John 12:32].[23]

The Christian life blooms and flourishes in the light of God's glory, where God both gives *out* and draws *in*. Having received new life in Christ from God's glorious grace, we find ourselves drawn in to enjoy him and to long for more of him.

> We expect that as we grow in grace we shall behold more and more of God's glory; but we shall see it best in the Well-beloved, even in Christ Jesus our Lord. What a sight of God we shall enjoy in heaven! We are tending that way, and, as we get nearer and nearer, our sight and vision of the glory of God in Christ is every day increased.[24]

Rooted in glory, and gravitating to glory: that, according to Spurgeon, is the nature of the Christian life.

---

[20] *MTP*, 25:511.
[21] *MTP*, 25:511.
[22] *MTP*, 25:511–12.
[23] *MTP*, 25:511.
[24] *MTP*, 25:513.

GENERAL INDEX

SCRIPTURE INDEX

WISDOM FROM THE PAST
FOR LIFE IN THE PRESENT

Theologians on the Christian Life

AUGUSTINE
by GERALD BRAY

BAVINCK
by JOHN BOLT

BONHOEFFER
by STEPHEN J. NICHOLS

CALVIN
by MICHAEL HORTON

EDWARDS
by DANE C. ORTLUND

LEWIS
by JOE RIGNEY

LLOYD-JONES
by JASON MEYER

LUTHER
by CARL R. TRUEMAN

NEWTON
by TONY REINKE

OWEN
by MATTHEW BARRETT AND
MICHAEL A. G. HAYKIN

PACKER
by SAM STORMS

SCHAEFFER
by WILLIAM EDGAR

SPURGEON
by MICHAEL REEVES

WARFIELD
by FRED G. ZASPEL

WESLEY
by FRED SANDERS

The Theologians on the Christian Life series provides accessible
introductions to the great teachers on the Christian life, exploring their
personal lives and writings, especially as they pertain to the walk of faith.

Visit crossway.org/TOCL for more information.